D1527235

THE BOSS CLUB

7 WINNING LEADERSHIP TECHNIQUES EVERY
FEMALE NEEDS IN BUSINESS AND THE WORKPLACE.
CONQUER GENDER BIAS, BUILD CONFIDENCE, AND
GET THE RESPECT YOU DESERVE.

DAHLIA CALLUM

CONTENTS

Just For You!

Free Gift To Our Readers

Learn the 5 mistakes made by CEOS of the world's top companies and how to avoid them. Visit: www.dahliacallum.com

INTRODUCTION

"I'm no longer accepting the things I cannot change. I am changing the things I cannot accept."

— ANGELA DAVIS

"Congratulations, it's a girl!"

From the moment you open your eyes to this world, you have an invisible list of expectations to meet . . .

The perfect daughter,
The caring wife,
The responsible daughter-in-law.

But who do YOU want to be? Maybe you don't want yourself to be limited to these roles but rather stand out. Some might think you're working hard to prove your worth to the world. But is it really about that? Only you know that what you crave isn't recognition but acceptance. For the woman you were yesterday, the woman you are today, and the woman you will be tomorrow.

You try to prove your managerial and leadership skills over your male colleagues by going overboard. You try to prove that you're more efficient at your job, which causes you to suffer from burnout, depression, and anxiety.

Am I good enough?

This is a question I know many women have been plagued with, as I often asked myself this in my previous job as a manager in a male-dominated industry. I know I'm not the first person who has ever doubted her capabilities; unfortunately, I won't be the last.

You've probably noticed how gender influences the ethics, values, and policies of several businesses and workplaces today. You may have also observed how discrimination against female managers and leaders has increased over time and caused inequality in the corporate world.

It's widely known that women have strong social and interpersonal skills. We are also great at multitasking, communicating, and working with teams, and several studies have shown that these skills make us natural leaders and managers. But, sadly, it's hard for us to grow into this potential, as the organizational system today is gendered.

Our gendered society and gendered institutions have stunned the growth of women. We, women, have minds that can speak louder and thoughts that can revolutionize industries. Even though the number of women in senior leadership roles is increasing worldwide, we still need help to attain top management levels.

Equal rights form the basis of feminism. Yet, we are far from achieving the significant agendas. From benevolent sexism to institutionalized fear of being radicalized, women have experienced trauma on diverse levels. Sexism and patriarchy have been embedded within several organizations around the globe. Why else would it be that while women make up 47% of the workforce, only 40.9% of managers are female? The percentage falls further as we move up the corporate hierarchy, dwindling to 4% for female CEOs. The statistics are even less favorable for women of color.

A 2020 research analysis of over 1,100 organizations worldwide by Mercer, the world's largest outsourced asset management firm, found that only 23% of women are executives. The report also revealed that the shares of female executives, senior managers, managers, professionals, and support staff were 23%, 29%, 37%, 42%, and 47%, respectively.

Consequently, as you can see, there's a leaky pipeline for women in leadership, as we're mostly denied executive and middle management positions.

Well, there is some good news as well. For instance, in 2021, women's roles in senior management increased globally by 31%; thus, 90% of companies worldwide have employed at least one woman in their senior management roles by 2021.

Leadership roles have been shifting for women. Women have started taking on leadership roles such as CEO, CFO, and CIO instead of only staying within the HR director zone. Simultaneously, Fortune Global 500 reported an increase in women CEOs, an all-time high of twenty-three women as CEOs, which included six women of color.

These statistics are not all bad. But what is important is that we understand the underlying problem. It's not that women do not have opportunities; it's that these opportunities are limited in many countries and states. They also come with the price of sexism that is ingrained within our society and organizational systems.

It is not just enough for women to prove their worth in a system rigged against them. It is time for a radical system change.

Having realized how the corporate world stifles women, I'm now inspired to help my fellow female leaders and aspiring boss ladies. I want to help us women regain our confidence and prove to everyone that we are more than qualified to lead.

I believe the only way to change the system is by having more women in leadership roles . . . and why is that? Because female bosses are less likely to discriminate based on gender, as they have first-hand experience and know what it is like to be underestimated based solely on their gender.

I have worked in both a female-led company and a male-led company and was shocked by the difference in approaches and overall environment. In the female-led company, employees were more accepting of each other. Men treated their female counterparts with more respect than when I worked in a male-run company.

This difference in overall behavior was rather infuriating.

Positions of power are still held primarily by men, even though women make up roughly half the population. Needless to say, many decisions impacting women directly are being made by men. This is why it is critical for more and more women to actively pursue leadership positions. It is time to take the reins of our destiny vigorously. We must become the narrators of our own stories if we wish to experience true liberty. The unseen barriers and the glass ceilings of society must be shattered to achieve greater equality for women.

What makes a woman a good leader?

The answer comes from the fact that women are taught from an early age to strike a work-life balance, making them much better managers. They are more empathetic and inclusive because they know what it is like to have the short end of the stick. Also, what have years of living in a patriarchal system earned us? Two World Wars, the threat of nuclear annihilation, a planet that is dying, and the various conflicts that exist in multiple parts of the globe. I wonder how different our world would have been if women had been in charge from the beginning.

The saddest part is that stereotypes exist even when there are no gender inequalities in one's leadership potential or job performance. According to research on gender stereotypes, the glass ceiling is an unseen barrier that prevents women from rising to top management and leadership levels in businesses. It mainly affects women, especially women of color, and more often in workplaces with more male workers than females.

My confidence became my superpower; it took me a few years to realize this, but it changed my life once I did. With my spiked confidence, I was able to enhance my performance. I was able to live up to my true potential, whether in terms of making a difficult decision or communicating effectively.

This can be you too.

Admittedly, it wasn't all plain sailing for me, especially when I discovered my real enemies: gender bias and toxic masculinity.

Although on the positive side, as these issues increased, so did the feminist movement and the awareness of women's involvement in the workplace. These movements aim to curb women's problems in the workplace, like unpaid salaries, low female representation in executive positions, and violence against women.

Yet, despite various efforts to fight them, these issues may not end anytime soon.

Therefore, women must take that bold step to overcome these challenges and be treated fairly in the workplace. And that is precisely what I did. I took the bull by the horns, and today I'm proud of what I have come to achieve for myself and my business.

Believe it or not, there is a hidden advantage of women in leadership. While technical expertise, experience, and knowledge are essential for success, employers now place much more value on soft skills. Soft skills are now regarded as "much more vital to work readiness," according to the Department of Labor.

Soft skills, also known as emotional intelligence, are aptitudes that affect how you interact with people or handle your professional life. These include crucial leadership abilities like the following:

- Being able to think critically and solve problems intuitively
- Being able to communicate effectively, both orally and in writing
- Professionalism (self-motivation, work ethic, resilience)
- The ability to network and collaborate

A study by the international consulting firm Hay Group found that women outperform men in eleven of twelve crucial emotional intelligence competencies, demonstrating that women hold a significant advantage in these soft skills. One of the study's developers and co-owners, Richard E. Boyatzis, Ph.D., asserts that "if more men behaved like women in employing their emotional and social competencies, they would be significantly and distinctly more effective in their work."

That's right, so you better believe it!

In addition to these capabilities, we can build trust and handle challenges well, especially when acting fast in crises. Our innate maternal instinct means we can resolve arguments, work in teams, and foster cooperation. These are the skills we learn naturally because navigating life as a female is full of challenges, which make us strong in our will and action.

So, yeah, you've got to lead like the boss you are!

In an organization, the toxic culture might entrap you into a position that would make you question your confidence and true potential.

You may ask yourself questions like the following:

"What if I don't meet the expectations of my superiors, who always underestimate me and my capabilities because I am a woman?"

"How do I fight sexism, discrimination, and gender bias in my workplace, as I am tired of constantly trying to prove myself?"

"How do I get my bosses and coworkers to respect me in my workplace?"

"And how do I regain my confidence, learn the best leadership skills, and improve myself in my lacking areas?"

If you've repeatedly asked yourself these questions, I want you to know that you aren't alone. The truth is that several women, including me, have experienced these challenges in the workplace.

And let's face it: this isn't the first time you would try to change your situation, climb the corporate ladder, and explore real leadership opportunities. Or is it?

So what's holding you back?

Perhaps it's because too much information on female leadership in the workplace is scattered across various pages on the internet, making it impossible to learn about everything you need to know.

Well, whatever that is, while reading this book, you'll discover seven winning leadership methods you can easily use in your workplace and business to earn your colleagues' and bosses' respect. So, rather than surfing the internet and browsing ten tabs simultaneously to find the proper guidance for your leadership mindset, you can use this book as a one-stop resource for everything that concerns female leadership in business and the workplace.

Now, you may wonder, *how can I become a successful female boss? Are there any requirements?*

The truth is the traits of being a great leader are the same regardless of gender. However, you might need these components in slightly more significant quantities than men to compensate for not having the Y-chromosome.

And that's where this book comes in.

Let me help you channel your inner goddess and help revive these true potentials in you.

The Boss Club will do just that. This book is a complete guide that explores women and challenging workplace environments. It equips female leaders, managers, and employers in business and the workplace with exemplary leadership techniques.

In the end, you'll achieve the following:

- Have a clearer understanding of how to thrive in a male-dominated corporate world.
- Learn the seven strategies to help you deal with workplace toxicity and discrimination, improve negotiation skills, and develop emotional intelligence.
- Create a framework that serves as a roadmap and memory jogger to help you assess your strengths and weaknesses and fulfill managerial responsibilities.
- Understand how to develop critical leadership qualities to thrive in your workplace and business.
- Discover strategic approaches to help reduce stereotypes about women in male-populated careers. Ultimately, you will learn how to conquer gender bias and build self-confidence.

Moreover, this book will show you how to become a successful female who commands respect anywhere she goes.

In this book, you will gain insights into the leadership techniques several other women like you and I have used and are still using to climb the corporate ladder.

You can immediately use these techniques to transform your professional and personal life.

We are all ladders for each other, and with my support, I can make sure that any woman who reads this book is a role model too!

As we get into this book, I advise you to prepare yourself because making a change will take some deliberate effort. You'll have to take action and work hard to get your desired results. Although it may be challenging since you're trying something new, I promise it'll be worth it. I also recommend passing along these techniques you'll learn from the book so we can all grow together as female leaders striving toward our goals and joining the Boss Club.

Are you feeling excited about the journey already?

Well, then, let's get started!

1

BECOMING A BOSS WOMAN

"I have broken many glass ceilings, so I know it can be done."

— HELEN CLARK

W hat are the qualities of a successful female boss, and how can I become that?

How can I navigate being a leader to people who were once my peers?

Will they respect and listen to me?

These were some of the questions I asked myself constantly when I got promoted to a managerial posi-

tion. Sure, I was excited about making more money—
who wouldn't be? But I was anxious and nervous about
being in that role. I was friends with all my colleagues,
and I knew that with my new role, I had to shift gears
and transition into a leader they would want to listen to
and follow.

This was a difficult task for me as I worked in a male-
dominated industry and was the only female boss in
that position. I hence immediately felt inferior to all the
male testosterone in the office.

With the different stereotypes about female leaders
today, I realized I didn't have to succeed by going over
the top with my female charms or adopting the domineering traits men often display in the workplace. So
what was my secret? It wasn't until I tapped into my
self-confidence and trusted my capabilities—which
landed me the promotion in the first place—that I
started gaining the strength I needed to excel as a
leader. Confidence is a vital leadership technique that
you need to have as a female boss, which is why there is
a chapter specifically dedicated to that to be discussed
in more detail.

It was also easy to be inspired and motivated as a leader
when a female owned the company. I always thought it
was badass that a female owned the company and
exemplified what a true boss woman is supposed to be

and how others looked up to her. The work environment was nontoxic, and my coworkers treated me with respect. I had no reason to think or complain about gender bias or toxicity in the workplace. It wasn't until I worked at another company in the same industry owned by a male that I noticed some changes. I was treated differently from my male counterparts. I experienced most of the exclusions from managers' meetings, my opinions being overlooked and under-addressed, and not getting the respect and accolades I deserved.

It made me question why gender bias and toxic masculinity existed in the company. It also led me to think that having a woman boss makes a big difference in how females are treated in the workplace. It's easier to approach a female boss with sensitive questions or requests. This is because we care about our team, well-being, work performance, and work-life balance.

Women have played a key role in shaping history and culture for many years; we have also paved the path for business leaders and entrepreneurs in every industry. Female leaders are passionate about their visions and goals. We stir others into action to achieve our mission and inspire change through our words and deeds. This is why I want to start by discussing the qualities of a successful female leader.

It's essential to understand how much creativity and resilience reside inside you. When you do, you'll create unique stories that illustrate the ultimate force of your womanhood and transform your life.

WOMEN ARE GREAT LEADERS

Contrary to popular belief, your input is vital to your company's or business's success as a woman. For instance, several organizations prioritize specific soft skills for strengthening employee relationships, like communication, team building, and multitasking. And women seem to possess these skills innately.

Naturally, women think about how to boost morale and encourage better workplace relations. A good example is General Motors Co, led by Mary Barra as the CEO, which developed a policy of providing hourly employees with profit-sharing payments to help secure a strong future. In fact, eligible hourly employees have earned over $70,000 each in profit sharing since 2015, earning the company a reputation for looking after its employees.

Despite gender bias and toxic masculinity, many women are stepping up today. Moreover, they outperform men in similar positions by helping their teams manage work-life challenges better, ensuring their well-being. Women leaders also outdo men in DEI (diversity, equity, and inclusion) initiatives. According to a report by McKinsey & Company, senior-level women are twice as likely as senior-level men to allot time for such activities at least once a week.

As you can see, women undoubtedly make great leaders. We have the abilities and untapped potential that organizations must start to unravel. Although we may not always realize how poised for success we are in leadership roles, our potential and skills are undeniable. Below are the top reasons women make great leaders:

- **We lead by example:** All female business leaders have something in common; they lead by example. They are not afraid to show others that walking off the beaten path is okay. They lead boldly by sharing their experience and personal lessons and writing or speaking out.
- **We communicate effectively:** Survey results from supervisors and subordinates have shown that people believe women are better at communicating with others and being considerate. Compared to men, women use more transformational leadership (inspiring, caring, and encouraging) and more contingent reward behaviors.

- **We value work-life balance:** Women leaders are great at balancing personal and professional leadership roles, which includes recruitment and retention of the valuable workforce, reduced employee stress, job satisfaction, reduced absenteeism, health benefits, and better life balance. And this is because we care about our team and their well-being.
- **We focus on teamwork:** Several studies have confirmed that women are more likely to care for the collective, meaning we're likelier to step in when we see a gap or ambiguity. While men believe that being a good team player is knowing your position and playing it well, women agree that helping their colleagues get things done is the true definition of a good team player.
- **We're good at multitasking**: Studies have shown how men and women achieve similar results when they tackle tasks one at a time. However, women performed better when the jobs were mixed up and made fewer mistakes as the assignments got more intense. And this isn't so surprising since women are natural multitaskers who stay more organized when under pressure.

- **We're more inclusive:** Women bring diversity and a different perspective to their workplaces. For instance, when companies face problems, getting more women involved in decision-making positions equips businesses with various solutions and alternatives men may not have thought of. Ultimately, that gives companies more problem-solving possibilities.
- **We have high emotional intelligence:** Women's brains are hardwired to focus more on the emotional nature of things and nurture the emotional space. In contrast, men's brains focus more on noticing emotion and turning it to find a solution. Hence, women can recognize emotions both in themselves and others.
- **We're more empathetic:** Women actively see the world through other people's eyes. We don't just listen to form an answer; instead, we listen keenly to what a person is saying verbally and through their body language, which makes us compassionate and strong.
- **We're motivated by challenges:** Women accept challenging roles as we're inspired by self-fulfillment and the need to become economically independent. We hardly take "no" for an answer.

- **We handle crises well:** Women are gifted caretakers who can handle crises excellently. We don't wait until problems become severe before attending to them, nor do we shirk our responsibilities in critical situations.

In the end, as leaders, women can influence others to achieve common goals. We naturally possess skills that help us motivate, communicate goals effectively, and offer support when needed to ensure the well-being of those around us. We can wear many hats, be open to new ideas and others' opinions, and keep our egos in check while carrying out our duties effectively.

TRAITS OF POWERFUL FEMALE BOSSES

Saying strong female bosses are essential is an understatement, no matter what kind of business or industry one is functioning in. Female bosses are needed not only for offering a much-required perspective on an organization's course but also for the traits they bring to the table, which are hard to come by otherwise.

I would love to share eight critical traits of a strong female leader. Recognizing these traits and their relevance is the key to developing the winning leadership techniques you need to excel in the workplace. That said, below are the eight essential qualities every influential female leader must have:

- **Strength:** Powerful female bosses have the strength to take risks, learn from failure, and deal with criticisms, insults, or gender stereotypes. They're bold to fight for what they believe is right and will never give up, regardless of how challenging the situation is. You thus have to be strong enough to believe in yourself, even when surrounded by people who think less of you. J. K. Rowling's story of rags to riches is one of the many stories showing a woman's strength and courage.
- **Perseverance:** Several women leaders have shown their abilities to learn and stay true to their goals despite uncertainty. This is what perseverance is all about. Generally, perseverance is the attribute of the strong, the theme of the female bosses who won't take "no" for an answer, and the mantra of those women who keep on pushing, even after they stumble and fall.
- **The ability to create women-empowered workplaces:** Although female bosses have the same traits as their male counterparts—vision, perseverance, empathy, passion, etc.—what sets

them apart is their ability to create genuinely women-empowered workplaces.

- **Adaptability:** Female leaders are an excellent fit for a work environment or position with unique demands, as we tend to adapt quickly. And this is an important attribute, especially today when these demands constantly evolve in business and the workplace. Thus, adaptability helps female leaders endure these changes and use them to their advantage.

- **Knowing how to ignore bad advice:** You'll agree that being able to ignore bad advice, especially without making the adviser feel remorse, is a valuable skill worth learning. Usually, female bosses can keep moving forward, sticking to their plans, and getting to know their company, industry, and buyers better while ignoring advice from people who lack the relevant knowledge to guide them. This means that to win as a female boss, you should only be getting advice from people with more experience in whatever you're working on.

- **Grit:** Grit is passion mixed with perseverance to achieve long-term goals. Since our business world is filled with uncertainty, which creates distractions and causes stress, having this trait will help you as a leader to thrive and succeed in the long term. Jessica Matthews, CEO of Uncharted Power, is an excellent example of a female boss who exemplifies grit. After several attempts at creating energy-capturing products, Matthews didn't give up. Instead, she pressed on until she made her breakthrough. Today, the company enables energy capture tech within various manufacturers' products.

- **Knowing how to ask:** Strong female bosses are adept at asking what they need to succeed. Instead of giving in to the circumstances or hoping that someone else will notice and remove the obstacles, you should take charge of the situation yourself. That's how you'll grow to become the most powerful player in the room. Sheryl Sandberg, former COO of Meta Platforms, and Arianna Huffington are examples of female leaders that exhibit this trait.

- **Tenacity:** Women in leadership frequently confront obstacles that men never do. Many are family-oriented, and some may see joyful personal experiences like pregnancies and maternity breaks as debilitating to the workplace's drive. Because of these factors, female managers must project confidence and tenacity in their professional endeavors. These additional obligations don't warrant excluding businesswomen because they are "delicate" or preoccupied. Instead, they demonstrate our capacity for weight and leadership in all spheres of life.

Studying the psychology of leadership and what makes successful women different from others is interesting, and you've got to be bold. So take a stand and believe in yourself. And if you fail, simply try again. You shouldn't be afraid to ask for help when needed. Then, in the end, you'll be surprised to see how far you've come as a boss woman.

HABITS OF SUCCESSFUL WOMEN

Before we continue, let's do a quick exercise. I want you to close your eyes for a few seconds and imagine what a successful woman looks like.

Tell me, who did you envision?

Was it a public figure, someone you know, or an imaginary woman?

Whoever it was, I want you to hold on to that image.

Usually, there's more than meets the eye when it comes to success. And as women, great habits are integral to many aspects of our lives, from living in a way aligned with our core values to finding success in our respective careers.

Forming good habits—and breaking bad ones—can be the very thing that drives us faster toward our dream destination. So let's delve into the habits every successful woman has in common:

- **They're a morning person:** Successful women are usually the morning type. I love to wake up around 5 a.m., and the effects are amazing. I wasn't too enthusiastic about getting up early at first, but I loved it once I began to see its benefits. You can focus on work during the first few hours of the day by waking before everyone else in your home. You shouldn't be concerned about answering emails, returning calls, or managing your social calendar until later in the day.
- **They set goals and stick to them:** Successful businesswomen have lofty aspirations but short-term objectives. While it's necessary to keep an eye on the future, completing your daily tasks is even more important. So try to create goals at the beginning of each week.

After that, list your top priorities and plan your daily duties. As you do this, you'll be closer to attaining your long-term objectives with each short-term goal you achieve.

- **They prioritize important tasks first:** Some days, you'll feel like you have too many tasks to complete. This is normal, and I've been there myself. But the secret is to organize your duties in order of importance. Starting each day with creative activities enables me to devote my best energy to the areas that demand it the most. So I don't deal with customer inquiries, orders, meeting scheduling, etc., until later in the day.

- **They never stop reading or learning:** If you're a female boss, consider relevant knowledge and information your weapon; you can never have enough. Since the internet became widely accessible in the 2000s, there is almost nothing you can't learn. So to become a better leader, read books related to your area of interest and stories of other successful female leaders.

- **They track their finances:** Keeping a close eye on your finances will help you to understand your financial standing at any time. It is important to manage your money and ensure you take the necessary steps to protect your future.

- **They practice gratitude:** This is more personal for me, as I'm most grateful for my life-changing experiences. One way to practice gratitude is to write down at least three things you're grateful for daily. Doing this will remind you of your wins and blessings, which can motivate you on difficult days.
- **They make exercise a priority:** As I've learned from experience, it's easy to fall into the trap of putting work above anything else as a businesswoman or corporate executive. But do you know one thing you can't give up? Your well-being. You can only invest in your mental and physical health if you first focus on your physical well-being. That way, you won't experience burnout.

Finally, I've discovered that successful women see mistakes and failures as learning experiences. Indeed, I've made many mistakes in the past, like failed business ventures, relationships wearing thin, etc. But what matters most is that I learned from my mistakes and made sure not to repeat them. While you can't change the past, you can always work to change the future.

TOO MANY GLASS CEILINGS

Women's careers aren't just being talked about in the media; they're also addressed frequently by governments worldwide, on the front pages of newspapers, inside glitzy magazines, on the radio, and online.

Amazingly, there's so much buzz around women and their careers, as people are talking about women's rights at work, and attitudes are changing. As a result, things are getting exciting for women at work, especially recently.

However, if you look at gender-split job statistics, the situation is pretty much as depressing as it has always been. From corporate boardrooms to Congress, health-care companies to the courts, and nonprofit organizations to universities, we see more men than women rising to these top roles.

Although women outnumber men in earning bachelor's and master's degrees and comprise about half of the U.S. labor force, we still don't get the highest-paying and most prestigious leadership and top management positions.

You might be wondering why . . . It's because factors qualifying employees for leadership positions are still based on the age-old stereotype that men alone should be leaders. Unfortunately, women haven't made much progress in breaking this stereotype, even after decades of increased awareness about gender equality and investment in women's leadership programs.

Today, there are still many barriers to women's leadership, but below are the most common ones:

1. Old stereotypes

Many studies consider stereotypes a major force impacting women's ability to advance in an organizational setting. Today, four conditions in the workplace facilitate stereotypes and the biased decision-making it produces:

- First, men have dominated leadership roles for so long that when women demonstrate leadership qualities, they aren't as well received.
- Second, when people don't have crucial information on how results were achieved, they tend to interpret them to conform to stereotypes, mainly that women are less capable than men. The more inference required to evaluate performance, the more stereotypical biases creep in.
- Third, evaluations become subjective when criteria for measuring performance, which leads to pay raises and promotions, are not well

defined. Stereotypical biases sneak in when subjectivity is involved in performance, pay, and promotions decisions.

- Fourth, stereotypes increase when performance cannot be unequivocally attributed to one individual. A woman's success is often explained away by factors other than skill, such as luck; other times, it is attributed to someone else entirely.

2. Fewer "connections"

Men continue to have more networks than women, allowing them to easily access opportunities and locate mentors and sponsors who will support their growth.

3. Bias and discrimination

Besides gender stereotypes, women still face other issues in the workplace, like sexual harassment, toxic work conditions, and hidden biases. Women of race encounter more barriers to success and are thus even less likely to assume leadership positions.

Unfortunately, when only a few women hold leadership positions, the likelihood that bias and discrimination will come into play increases. And this is true for anyone who is a minority.

4. Lack of flexibility

The difficulty juggling work and home obligations sometimes prevent women from pursuing leadership positions. The outdated idea of gender roles in the home is still used in the workplace.

For instance, how often does a woman say something in a meeting, yet no one acknowledges it? Then a few minutes later, a man says the same thing, and people agree he has made an excellent point.

Attributing good work to someone else is particularly relevant given the emphasis on teams in organizations; generally, teams obscure each member's contributions.

As you can see, there are just too many glass ceilings. And although these stereotypes and barriers are old as dirt, the dirt is tough to eliminate.

So, where does that leave us?

How do we break through female stereotypes and other barriers and become successful female leaders?

We will focus on that in the next chapter and beyond. Indeed, women deserve the same respect, pay, and job titles as our male peers.

As women, we want equality, but we also want something more than that—we want to stay uniquely and wonderfully female. The same pay, yes. Opportunities, of course. But we don't want to abandon our femininity at the office's revolving door. Gender parity does not imply gender uniformity. As a passionate and vibrant woman, I embraced my distinctive peculiarities, and so should you.

In essence, my message in the next chapter is based on the idea that while everyone deserves to be treated equally at work, women must understand the different leadership styles, find the one that works for them, and use it to make an impact in the workplace and business.

2

LEADERSHIP STYLES AND HOW TO FIND YOUR OWN

"Do what you feel in your heart to be right–for you'll be criticized anyway."

— ELEANOR ROOSEVELT

How would you reply if someone asked you what leadership means?

You should consider your response carefully since it will show what type of leader you are or wish to be and the leadership stances you want to take.

While different leadership styles exist, your preferred style will depend on your personality and how you want to manage your team. So, naturally, you will know more about the leadership styles that work best for groups and organizational processes the longer you lead your team.

Your leadership style determines how you influence others and how your actions affect your organization or division's overall success. Although some people are natural leaders, anyone can become a leader by embracing the lessons leaders share and then intro-specting to understand how their behavior affects others. Good leaders also understand the need to improve their leadership style constantly.

You can significantly enhance your impact in your workplace by understanding the different leadership styles. But to help you understand your influence as a leader, let us first define leadership, explore what a leadership style is, and discuss the different leadership styles and how to find yours.

WHAT IS A LEADERSHIP STYLE?

Leadership in the workplace is the practice of inspiring team members to work together toward a common goal. It is based on concepts that may be one's own or those of other influential figures. Effective leadership involves a leader motivating themself and those they lead. Along with guiding the organization toward growth, effective leadership also involves successfully conveying ideas to others and inspiring them to take on responsibilities and develop personally.

A leadership style refers to a leader's behavior and approach when directing, motivating, and managing others. Your leadership style also affects how you develop and execute plans while considering your team's needs and stakeholders' expectations.

Understanding your leadership style is crucial because it tells how you impact people directly under your leadership. Every leadership approach has weaknesses, enabling you to proactively address areas that need improvement. This is important since some workers might be reluctant to participate in an anonymous survey, which could make it hard to determine the weaknesses of the leadership style.

TYPES OF LEADERSHIP STYLES

Although many leadership styles exist, I will share the most common ones below:

1. Democratic leadership

Democratic leadership is precisely what the name implies: the leader makes decisions based on every team member's input. It is also referred to as participative or facilitative leadership. Every team member can participate equally in the decision-making process, although the leader makes the final decision.

Democratic leadership is effective in business because it is similar to how decision-making usually occurs in board meetings. In a company board meeting, for instance, a democratic leader would present the team with a few options under consideration. Then they might discuss different aspects of each choice. Afterward, this leader may put the matter to a vote or consider the board's opinions and suggestions before finally deciding what to do.

However, the democratic style poses some potential challenges for leaders. For instance, consensus-building requires so much time, money, and communication. Also, decision-making may be affected since certain team members need more knowledge to make meaningful decisions.

2. Autocratic leadership

Authoritarian, coercive, or commanding leadership are other terms for autocratic leadership. This leadership style is considered the antithesis of democratic leadership because leaders make decisions without consulting those they lead.

Businesses benefit from autocratic leadership since team members give their all to strategies and orders. Likewise, better performance may result from this style because no employees are notified before a change in direction. Instead, employees are expected to follow the decision at the leader's set time and pace.

But as time-saving and effective as this leadership style is, it has some drawbacks. For instance, most businesses today can't maintain a dominant culture without losing workers. Unfortunately, employees' morale and innovative problem-solving skills may suffer as a result. An illustration of this may be when a manager alters the shift times for staff members without seeking their input.

There is also the case of intimidation, micromanagement, and overreliance on a single leader with this leadership style.

3. Laissez-faire leadership

If you recall your high school French, you might have guessed that laissez-faire leadership is the least intrusive leadership style. Laissez-faire, a French expression, loosely translates to "let them do it." Leaders following this style delegate almost all authority to their staff. In fact, laissez-faire leadership is often referred to as hands-off or delegative leadership.

Employees are held accountable for their job by laissez-faire bosses. As a result, many employees will be motivated to give their work their best efforts. Furthermore, leaders practicing laissez-faire leadership foster a more casual business culture. Thus, the laissez-faire model is excellent for creative enterprises such as ad agencies or product design. It's also an excellent fit for a company with a highly skilled workforce.

For instance, a laissez-faire company founder at a budding startup would not set any significant office policies regarding work hours or deadlines. And while concentrating on the business's broader operations, they might have complete faith in their staff.

Workers for laissez-faire bosses feel valued because of this high level of trust. So they obtain the required data and use their resources and skills to achieve their business objectives.

Although allowing people to work however they see fit might empower them, laissez-faire leadership has several drawbacks. The most significant downside is that this leadership style may hamper your team's growth. In addition, inexperienced or new staff may be a major problem, which could cause you to miss important business growth opportunities.

So, it's essential to keep this leadership style in check.

4. Transformational leadership

Transformational leadership constantly "transforms" and upgrades the company's norms. Employees may have basic responsibilities and goals they must achieve weekly or monthly. Still, the leader continuously encourages them to push themselves outside their comfort zone.

Transformational leaders can motivate their teams to think differently. This can assist businesses in updating business processes to increase productivity and profitability. And this can often improve employee satisfaction and morale.

Transformational leaders, however, risk overlooking everyone's unique learning curves. So if you practice this style, ensure direct reports receive the proper coaching to help them navigate new obligations. Working with your team to update benchmarks is crucial because employee burnout can be another significant problem.

5. Coaching leadership

Leaders using this model focus on discovering and improving each team member's unique skills, much like a coach does for their sports team. Additionally, they focus on strategies that can promote team spirit. Democratic leadership shares many similarities with this method. However, the coaching model prioritizes the development and success of employees more than any other style. For instance, by giving workers new assignments to tackle, a manager with this leadership style can help them hone their skills and also inspire them to improve.

Leaders that actively encourage skill development and autonomous problem-solving are known as coaching leaders. They establish a solid organizational culture to achieve their challenging commercial goals. They also serve as important mentors and contribute to an organization's long-term goal, even after leaving a company.

The coaching leadership style offers leaders the ability to concentrate on high performance, but it also has potential downsides. For instance, the coaching approach might take a long time to develop individuals, and not all employees respond well to mentoring. In addition, this management approach needs time and perseverance and only fits with some corporate cultures.

DECIDING BETWEEN DIFFERENT LEADERSHIP STYLES

You need good instincts to be a leader, and many leaders base their leadership style on their habits and experiences. So you should start taking notes as you embark on your leadership journey. But before you start, note the difficulties or scenarios you would manage. You can become a more confident and capable leader this way. However, you should consider changing your strategy if things go differently than you had hoped.

Your habits and instincts will always influence your leadership style. But if you often find yourself in ambiguous leadership situations, consider other leadership styles. For instance, if you're an extrovert and your team includes a shy person, you should work on your active listening capabilities (more of that in Chapter 5).

Likewise, you might need to acquire new techniques to encourage, support, and motivate your team if you're an introverted leader managing outgoing team members.

There are many factors to consider when choosing the right leadership style for you, so figuring out where to begin can be challenging. However, the following steps will guide you if you are still deciding which leadership styles will work for you:

- **Learn about yourself:** Different people require different routes to self-discovery. Some people go through a phase of exploring new things and taking risks. Others may benefit from solitude, writing activities, and evaluating their strengths and limitations. Exercise and social interaction are two other ways to discover more about yourself. Still, whatever method you use, knowing yourself is a crucial first step in determining which leadership style will work for you.

- **Describe your values and challenges:** Knowing yourself could help you better understand your priorities and challenges. As you will learn in Chapter 4, being a leader often entails working swiftly and making decisions immediately. So it pays to know your values in these situations. Examine defining incidents in your life as you list your values. Next, search for patterns, people you connect with, and common themes. You should also combine related thoughts because your list could be lengthy. Your reactions, strengths, limitations, and a foundation for your fundamental values can all be seen in this framework.

- **Observe leaders you admire:** You could determine and even improve your leadership style by observing influential leaders. You should make notes while watching these leaders during meetings, client interactions, and presentations. Another strategy is to analyze their activities in light of a particular leadership stance. This makes it easier to determine their leadership style and whether it would be effective for you.

- **Try different leadership styles:** One last way to determine whether a leadership style is right for you is to experiment with various ones. Having a summary of each leadership style that interests you can be helpful. Review your notes before your next meeting to see how you may apply this communication technique to future meetings.

So, what's left?

Of course, you should explore these five leadership styles and see which fits you best. Once you've discovered your style, you can proceed to the next stage, which involves building your confidence in yourself and your ability to effectively make important and sometimes spontaneous decisions.

Being confident is crucial for you as a female leader. Therefore, you must lead confidently; that way, you won't doubt yourself or be afraid to make difficult decisions.

CONFIDENCE IS A WEAPON

"I can be changed by what happens to me. But I refuse to be reduced by it."

— MAYA ANGELOU

The biggest tennis event is perhaps the one where Billie Jean King, a former world No. 1 female tennis player, accepted a challenge to play against Bobby Riggs, a former world No. 1 male tennis player. The event, which took place on September 20, 1973, was dubbed the "Battle of the Sexes" and had 50 million Americans glued to their TV screens.

King took a step into the unknown on that day. She took on a challenge from a physically bigger and stronger opponent, Riggs, who had several barbarous opinions against women then. He had boasted that women were inferior, couldn't handle the pressure of the game, and that, despite his age, he would beat any female player.

However, on the event day, King confidently walked onto the tennis court and played the game majestically. She remarkably thrashed Riggs, as she won in straight sets: 6–4, 6–3, 6–3.

"I thought it would set us back 50 years if I didn't win that match," King said. "It would ruin the women's tour and affect all women's self-esteem."

King had an overdose of self-confidence that day; more than that, she recognized and shouldered the supposed weakness of her female peers. And by doing so, King led them to a new place of bravado and belief.

You see, confidence is a state of mind. And no one is born confident, not even men. Instead, confidence evolves and influences how we change and shape our lives—just like the alpha female. The alpha female embraces her leadership ambitions, makes self-confidence a must-have personality trait, becomes a better leader, and thus excels in any aspect of life. You'll need to develop your confidence to become that fierce female leader.

In this chapter, I'll share how you can become more confident. We'll start by understanding self-confidence and how you can build it.

SELF-CONFIDENCE AND ITS IMPORTANCE

Theoretically, self-confidence is the feeling or belief that you can succeed at something. Self-confidence is so crucial that it's the bedrock for other winning leadership techniques in this book. It's also the cornerstone on which we build our careers.

Practically, self-confidence isn't just believing or feeling good and happy and walking into your workplace with a spring in your step; it's multifaceted. Self-confidence enables you to turn your thoughts into action; without it, you'll begin to doubt your abilities. In such situations, you would think you aren't important, able, and worthy, so you marginalize your success.

In my work evaluating executives for senior leadership roles, I've discovered a set of behaviors essential to organizational success, including active coping and self-confidence.

Confidence makes the difference between grabbing those ideas in your head and putting them into action and sitting impassively at your desk, resentful of the status quo.

Confidence is wrapped up and stitched into every action you take at work; those awkward situations, scary eventualities, successes, failures, wins, losses, and everything in between, are each defined by how confident we were in that moment.

The Importance of Self-Confidence

Most women have active, analytical minds that overly criticize themselves, making it harder for them to be confident. So we talk down on ourselves. We overthink —and I mean *a lot*. Then, we let mental flaws seep in, stop taking chances, or don't even speak up when we should.

Unfortunately, I've seen this firsthand in many women I work with. These women are talented and good at what they do, as you also are. But the issue is that they lack confidence and don't trust themselves enough, and when a lack of confidence dominates, they become passive. No matter how hard and competent you work at your job, you will not perform optimally when this happens. Indeed, the downward spiral of lack of confidence is a speedy and dangerous fairground ride: when you don't believe in it, you hinder yourself from even attempting to do it.

Why Women Leaders Need Self-Confidence

Confidence is crucial in the workplace because it's the difference between our hopes and achievements—the missing link.

King believed she would defeat Riggs in the "Battle of the Sexes." If she had walked out onto the court without trusting herself and her abilities, she would not have tasted victory. That is the power of confidence.

The biggest obstacle to us pursuing our goals, making lifestyle changes, and sharing our thoughts with the world is the feeling that we aren't good enough. We hold ourselves back and remain in our comfort zones because of this lack of self-confidence, resulting in feelings of inadequacy, low self-esteem, and a lack of drive and ambition.

We underestimate our abilities and hold back from applying for the perfect job or making that important business move. But behind that door could lie the most significant breakthrough you would never have imagined.

And for some of us who even try to take action, we often misattribute our success to luck when something goes right at work or in our business.

But it's hardly ever luck. No, far from it.

You were the one who put in the effort and made things happen; you just needed to be more confident to recognize your ability. So if you want to become a good leader, you've got to trust yourself and your abilities because that's the only way you can win in your business and workplace. The more you trust that you can do it, the more you'll try and realize that you *can* do it and so much more.

SECRETS TO CONFIDENCE FOR EVERY WOMAN LEADER

When we talk about the need for confidence and how to build it, many women find it a big deal for them. As I explained earlier, confidence is a state of mind. Sadly, you can't buy it over the counter, but I've got you. I'll share with you the secrets to strengthen your foundations. It's a crazy world out there, so it's OK to accept some guidance now and again.

Our counterparts in the workplace might appear showy and consider themselves the peacocks of the organization. Still, chances are they're no more talented than us peahens. Male employees are good at putting on a good show; they make us believe they are great at their jobs, and we succumb to their charms.

But the truth is, their confidence is just bravado and shimmer. Men excel at exuding strong, persuading confidence, so we can't criticize them. What's more intriguing is that confidence isn't a constant trait. Instead, it has a switch you can activate when things appear bleak or uncertain.

Since we all have insecurities, confidence is difficult for all sexes. But then, men tend to doubt themselves less often and are less likely to let it interfere with their work. Women's main issue is that we tend to falter even more when faced with all this macho resolve.

Therefore, we must learn to contend with the annoying voice in our minds (a big culprit of low confidence). But we need tools to manage the impact and know when those around us are brimming with confidence or acting all cool to keep it together. And that's exactly what I want to reveal to you.

Cultivate an Inner Champion

The inner voice that women choose to listen to is one significant influence we can manage. Everyone has an inner critic who is always ready to point out their mistakes or why they aren't good enough.

However, we can also cultivate an inner champion, a supportive voice that constantly reminds us of our successes and all our difficulties. A voice that says, "Don't hold back. You've come too far to give up."

Recognizing when the inner critic appears is the first step. But what does your inner champion have to say in response? Instead of accepting everything your inner critic says as accurate, consider whether her advice is genuinely helpful. If it's not beneficial, then decide not to listen.

Afterward, foster an inner champion. Apply the exact encouraging words to yourself that you would say to a friend who needs them.

Let Go of the Need to Be Perfect

In this war for female leadership, perfectionism is the enemy. It makes us risk-averse, kills our confidence, and congests production channels.

Although not all of us obsess about being perfect, many women do. We take pride in doing things nicely and correctly; worse yet, we wallow in our past imperfections and project them into our future.

But the truth is that we humans are imperfect. Those successful business leaders you see today are flawed too. Even those masters of sports, arts, and music you adore make mistakes or get rejected.

So you must learn to tame your perfectionism if you want to build confidence. And that's because we set ourselves free when we lower our self-imposed expectations.

You must also pick up those negative, intrusive thoughts —the *"I'm not good enough, I'm too old to learn, and I'm weak"*—and lock them behind a door inside your head.

Better yet, write them down on paper, then take great pleasure in tearing up the list of misplaced negative beliefs and dumping it in the bin. That way, you unbridle your brain from those toxic thoughts so that it's free to be strategic, sparky, and—yes, you guessed it —confident again.

Lean into Values

You can start working toward achieving your career goals once you become more aware of what is essential to you.

Take Martha, for instance. This young woman knew she needed to get more new clients to grow her coaching program and earn more, but she doubted whether she could. She always wanted to be a role model for her son, which was the one thing she was truly passionate about.

Over time, she found the confidence to approach people and ask them to patronize her business. And as a result of her efforts, her company gained more clients, which significantly increased her confidence.

The first critical step in reaching your professional goals is determining what's holding you back. When we overcome these systemic and internal barriers and lean on our values, we contribute more value and excel in our business and the workplace.

Take Action

Entering the risk zone and stepping outside your comfort zone is another excellent way to boost your confidence. Conquering a task increases self-efficacy, which inspires confidence.

So you need to leave your comfort zone and make critical decisions to increase your image and gain exposure. You should also voice your opinions and speak up when you should, whether at meetings or presentations. Also, you should showcase your achievements when it matters.

Engage in challenging dialogues, communicate with leadership several layers above you, and express your thoughts clearly in large gatherings. Your perception of your ability and confidence grows when you face your worries and take action.

Of course, I know confidence can be a seesaw between you and your colleagues, just as it's a voice in your head, a physical performance, a state of mind, and a deep belief.

And that's why we will explore some of these secrets further in the remaining sections of this chapter. Although it's a complex tool, it's one you can own and use, and it'll pay dividends once you master it.

CHAMPION AND MASTER YOUR INNER CRITIC

When I talk about the inner critic, I'm speaking about the voice in our heads—our inner voice.

Our inner voice can caution us when we're in danger or help us think more critically about something, but it can also be our worst enemy when it turns into a spiral of negative thoughts and emotions. And this is when our inner voice can become our inner critic.

Academic research has revealed that women generally have more self-doubt regarding activities stereotypically associated with men in our culture. These activities include mathematical work, negotiation, and traditional hierarchical leadership. These doubts can be disastrous to our careers and workplaces.

Below are some ways your inner critic can show up in your daily work life:

1. The imposter syndrome

Imposter feelings are feelings of self-doubt and personal incompetence in your capabilities at your job, even though you have the knowledge, expertise, and training required. Your inner critic may also prompt you to overanalyze things on repeat. It's even worse in these days of remote work, where the imposter syndrome has taken on new forms. For instance, you see women who attend Zoom meetings comparing themselves to others, thinking their colleagues are better than them and that they don't deserve to be at the same table. In such situations, you may feel you've deceived others into thinking you are someone you aren't.

2. The blame game

Your inner critic may tell you everyone knows more than you do, even when you're competent and knowledgeable. Or it may inhibit you from "showing weakness" by admitting that you know less about something than you genuinely do.

In the long run, you start to blame yourself for every-thing that goes wrong, whether or not it has anything to do with you.

3. The "do it all" fallacy

I've also seen many female professionals feel pressured to "do it all." But it's more important than ever to embrace the support of those around us and lift each other in times of stress or struggle.

You should tell yourself that no one—not even your employees—expects you to do it all. After all, that's why your team members have varying strengths and working styles to work with and support you and your initiatives.

At first glance, you may find it hard to believe that many women leaders have struggled with their inner critics and continue to do so, but it's true. They've only learned to master it.

And you, too, must do the same if you want to be a successful leader. So let's explore the different ways to champion and master your inner critic.

Learn to Trust Yourself

Learning to trust yourself and your intuition is an excellent way to silence your inner critic to enable you to hear what's true.

Take Carissa Moore, for instance. This first-ever female gold medalist in surfing in the Olympics has been candid about her battles with her inner critic. In an interview with *Surfer*, Moore cited her inner critic as the toughest challenge she had to overcome throughout her career, adding that she had learned to communicate with it.

"Yeah, I don't think that little self-doubt voice ever goes away," Moore told *USA Today*. "It's just learning to tell her, 'Hey, just be quiet for a little bit. I got this."

If you keep giving in to your inner critic, your negative thoughts may cause neuronal activity patterns that alter your brain's structure.

On the other hand, your brain becomes more wired to reason the more you learn to replace your inner critic with it. When you think logically, you are more forgiving of yourself and capable of seeing the nuances.

When Your Inner Critic Can Be Helpful

Create a character that personifies your inner critic. When you create a character with a name and visual image, you remind yourself that the critic is not your core; rather, it's one voice with its personality and pathology.

It's easier to get a handle on your inner critic because you can see its words as coming from a finite (and usually rather absurd) character. You can begin to have a sense of humor about the critic too. After all, what it says is usually ridiculous!

So when you hear the critic, ask that voice of self-doubt:

What are you trying to do right now?

What harm are you trying to protect me from?

Once you've created an inner critic character, you can picture your character and ask them in your mind's eye what their motivation is. You may also ask what they are so afraid of.

Once you've discovered the root of the critic's intentions, respond with compassion toward the critic's misguided attempt to keep you safe—usually from attack, embarrassment, isolation, or failure. You can do this by acknowledging those motives and sincerely responding with, "Thanks a lot for your input, but I've got this one covered."

Coach Your Inner Critic to Work for You

Most of us need to be more trained in differentiating the various voices we hear in our thoughts. We think they are all "us" in the same way. But no, they aren't!

You need to acknowledge your inner critic often. Name the inner critic voice when it shows up, then unbraid it from the other strands of "you," like your imagination, aspirations, and wisdom.

Here's how to coach your inner critic to work for you:

- **Notice and name it:** When you hear your critic talking, label this voice by simply saying to yourself, "Oh, I'm hearing my inner critic right now." By saying this, you can remember that's all it is and move forward despite its rants and threats. This is the foundational inner critic practice on which all the others depend.
- **Quiet the inner critic:** You can either stand up and "act out," walk your inner critic character into a different space or imagine them going to another place. Then, begin your work again, knowing it's just you there—your inner critic is on a break.
- **Don't let perfectionism hinder your progress:** Of course, you can have a perfect plan, but that doesn't mean you should obsess over perfection. Avoid perfectionism, and don't let your critic stop you from executing whatever task you have at hand. Instead, adjust the plan if needed. Sometimes, "fake it till you make it" is a necessary policy to get past our fear and

feelings of inadequacy until we learn to believe in ourselves.

- **Give yourself some credit:** It's easy to criticize ourselves but much harder to actually "be in the arena" solving problems, so give yourself the credit you deserve for putting yourself out there. For instance, when someone criticizes you constantly, which is their inner critic talking to you, you should flip it around and ask the person to tell you how to improve.

- **Find a mentor:** As a leader, it's essential to have someone to turn to when you struggle with your inner critic and need support. Finding a mentor is critical, whether inside or outside the organization. However, I recommend you talk to an industry expert outside your current organization to help you form a new mindset and gain perspective. In addition to finding a mentor, find the right tools and resources to inspire and help keep you in good shape.

If you start speaking to yourself how you would to a good friend or close colleague, you might realize your inner voice is no longer a harsh critic but a trusted confidant who will encourage you to fly.

So take hold of your career, grab it with both hands, and be proud of your opinion. When you become stronger and more confident, you will learn to accept that you didn't get to where you are today by luck. You are not a fraud, and you have secured your success.

THE DEAL WITH PERFECTIONISM

Defining "perfect" is almost impossible since there's no such thing as perfection. Whether or not something is perfect always depends on your point of view.

Yes, perfectionists aim to create flawless work and exhibit higher levels of drive and diligence than non-perfectionists. Some people argue that these traits of perfectionism can increase one's chances of success.

However, perfectionism starves confidence. It forces you to strive to be the best rather than work at your personal, realistic best. And I think it's a dirty little secret that most women looking to join the Boss Club are hiding.

Unfortunately, some women wear the perfectionist's badge with pride. It's a laminated name tag, all fresh and bright with smooth corners. However, when it comes to leadership, perfection can sometimes be both positive and negative—reaping the benefits of your labor and feeling that warm glow of success is exhilarating.

However, when perfection requires an exactness that's often impossible in business and the workplace, it becomes an anchor, pulling down the skills of a leader to be lost in the murky depths of micromanagement and tediousness. You'll hold yourself to unrealistically high standards for everything you care about if you're a perfectionist. With micromanagement, you'll make those under your constant, critical supervision feel oppressed and less apt to take risks or be creative and innovative with their job.

Logically, it's impossible to be perfect in all situations, all the time. Emotionally, as a perfectionist, you'll struggle to believe that until you become critical of yourself and others.

So breathe deeply, sisters. You have to let go of perfectionism to increase your effectiveness. Indeed, it's time you threw your perfectionism badge to the bottom of your purse because the risk is where the real fun lies.

Surround Yourself with People You Trust

As a boss woman, it would be best to have a team you can rely on to foster a supportive workplace atmosphere. So don't rush anything; be patient, and don't be afraid to follow your instinct.

It also significantly boosts your confidence to have a network of people who are prepared to help you as you pursue a leadership role. Having a network of peers, mentors, and coaches at different phases of their leadership path is very beneficial. Everyone has the option to assist others on their journey, and occasionally accepting assistance from others is also very helpful.

Look in the Mirror

You are doing others a disservice if you are always the first to point out a mistake (personally and professionally). If you constantly do things your way or have an all-or-nothing mindset, you should consult a health expert.

Perfectionism may be a risk factor for psychological disorders such as obsessive-compulsive disorder (OCD).

Understand When to Let Something Go

Sometimes, something may not be worthwhile. Avoid believing the "sunk cost fallacy," which is the notion that because you've already put in a lot of effort and time, you just need to put in a little more.

Being an effective leader means knowing when to give up and move on.

Become a More Authentic Version of Yourself

Nobody is flawless, so accept the sobering fact that you cannot manage every detail as a leader.

Learn to assign assignments to people you can trust and give them the room and flexibility to experiment and fail to come up with new solutions.

In addition, you should let the law of diminishing return guide you. In economics, the law of diminishing returns says that increasing labor at a certain point doesn't result in the same increase in productivity. Perfectionism has the significant drawback of making a leader reach this point of no return without realizing it, and extra effort doesn't provide better results. It doesn't imply that you should accept "good enough" for your task, but you should know that eventually, exerting more effort won't be fruitful.

OTHER STRATEGIES FOR IMPROVEMENT

It's key to remember that we are confident people in different dimensions of our lives. Also, we can extend this confidence to those aspects of our roles and careers where we are currently less assured.

Here are other strategies you can implement to build and boost your confidence:

- **Identify and leverage your strengths:** Knowing your strengths gives you a solid foundation for confidence. Usually, we can optimize our contributions if we take advantage of these strengths. Listing your talents and requesting feedback from your employer and perhaps other coworkers is beneficial. Offering to do this on a reciprocal basis with your peers can also be effective.
- **Address any "mission-critical" development areas:** Knowing exactly what you excel in will help you identify your areas of weakness. It's important to remember that despite your best efforts, you may not achieve the same level of success as if you had played to your strengths. However, it's critical to pinpoint the areas where you need to improve. Once more, look for fair criticism that identifies the fundamental aspects of your experience or ability that might prevent you from moving forward.
- **Realize that ambiguity is part of leadership:** Remembering that you are probably still doing a good job, even though you might experience some ambiguity and confusion, can be pretty

empowering. Many women find it challenging to transition from being a technical specialist (where they are on top of the details) to a more generalist role where you have to lead via others. A perspective shift and learning specific skills are pretty helpful in this situation. Understanding that uncertainty is a significant aspect of the leadership landscape and that learning to "know what to do when you don't know what to do" is also essential to effective leadership.

- **Find ways to make yourself strong:** Every person has a particular look or set of shoes that instantly boosts their confidence. Additionally, you may actively boost your impact and confidence when you stand tall, slow down, and control the pitch and tone of your voice.

- **Understand that leadership is a journey:** When we keep in mind that developing leadership skills takes time and necessitates stepping outside our comfort zone to continue improving, we get more confidence. If you subscribe to the growth mindset theory, which contends that intellect is dynamic, you'll seize opportunities to enhance your intelligence through education. In terms of leadership development, the same is true. You can

continue to learn throughout your leadership
journey by approaching leadership
development with a growth attitude.

Chances are we've all suffered from low confidence at
some point in our lives, and although it affects us
deeply, like many other leadership skills, it's also something we can overcome.

The ability to communicate with a wide range of individuals and the understanding that decision-making
skills must always be included as part of your vision—
not just in terms of leadership, but in all that we do—
are essential for leaders. So in the next chapter, we'll
discuss how to improve decision-making skills and
their importance in leadership. Get ready to stand
taller, transform yourself, and unearth your gravitas.

4

LEADERSHIP & DECISION-MAKING SKILLS

"The most difficult thing is the decision to act, the rest is merely tenacity. The fears are paper tigers. You can do anything you decide to do. You can act to change and control your life; and the procedure, the process is its own reward."

— AMELIA EARHART

Decisions, decisions . . . timely decisions. Every day, leaders are expected to make them and to make them right.

And when something implies you aren't a good decision-maker, you see it as a stain on your integrity. On the other hand, one of the highest accolades you can get in the workplace is when your colleagues describe you as a good decision-maker.

But what is decision-making, and what does it involve, especially since it's a necessary quality in the workplace?

We know we must make decisions in our everyday life. Which train should we board? Which school is best for our kids? Even when we're with our friends at the shopping mall, we're involved in decision-making— what outfit should we buy? And how would it match the items in our wardrobe?

Sometimes, we make these everyday decisions alone; other times, we consult our partners or friends first. Furthermore, these decisions can occur on a one-time basis, but at other times, there may be formal structures and rules or even unspoken traditions which guide our decision-making process.

The need for constant decision-making activities and recognition is evident in businesses and workplaces. Decision-making authority is defined or implicit in how the company is structured. For instance, almost everyone in the organization is expected to make certain decisions, and being a woman isn't an excuse.

Over time, I have realized that making the right decisions, whether big or small, is pivotal to the successful leadership of the female boss. The urge to solve a problem or seek a future opportunity drives decisions. Making educated decisions requires gathering the appropriate information and feedback from essential parties.

While decision-makers are expected to make routine decisions with minimal fuss at the lower levels, decisions are usually more complicated and require a degree of experience and judgment at the higher levels.

Some of these decisions are dealt with by individual managers, but groups of people usually deal with the more complex and intractable problems. The group might comprise senior managers or representatives of a broad range of expertise and interests, all of whom are leaders in the organization.

Regardless of who is responsible for the decision, be it an individual or a group, there are expectations that they will make decisions. So when they don't make the necessary choices, anguish and frustration ensue in the workplace. Indeed, employees probably feel more frustrated when decisions aren't made than when bad decisions are made. This is especially the case with the type of decision-making that occurs at an organization's highest level.

As a manager, leadership may require you to make decisions that impact colleagues and employees. So you must understand decision-making and how to acquire the skills to help you make tough and effective decisions.

This chapter delves into why decision-making is a must-have leadership skill and the strategies you can use to make good decisions in business and the workplace.

DECISION-MAKING: AN IMPORTANT LEADERSHIP SKILL

Decision-making is a leadership skill you can use to assess a situation or problem, make smart choices, and decide how the organization may proceed. Here's an overview of the decision-making process:

- **Identify the challenge:** In this step, you discover an issue and determine the circumstances that led to the situation.
- **Devise solutions:** After learning more about the case, you can create one or several possible solutions.
- **Weigh options:** Analyze the advantages and disadvantages of each option and explore alternative solutions if needed.

- **Make a choice:** Conduct a thorough assessment, then decide what action to take.
- **Inform others of the decision:** Inform employees of the decision and explain how the decision influences the workplace.

Why Decision-Making Is an Important Leadership Skill

As a leader in any organization, developing your decision-making skills is crucial. You'll need it when implementing new policies, setting and meeting organizational goals, developing new products, and building the brand.

Also, decision-making skills will help you recruit and train the right employees, design budgets, allocate financial resources, and enter new markets.

So let's explore four significant ways good decision-making skills can help you as a leader in the workplace and your business:

1. Workplace productivity will improve

Making effective decisions can save time and propel work projects forward, increasing productivity in the workplace.

For example, say you're a small fashion store manager, and your employees disagree about when to host the annual spring sale. This prevents the business from promoting the sale and preparing the store for an influx of customers. Then, after critical consideration, you decide the sale date should be April, and your employees immediately announce it.

Your decision will start the planning process and motivate employees to complete their associated occupational tasks. By doing this, the business won't stagnate but is sure to progress, and so will the employees.

2. Create better action plans in emergencies

Emergencies may require you to make quick, impactful decisions to minimize damage and optimize benefits.

For example, your workplace is located in a remote area, and it experiences a power outage, and the employees are now concerned with how the issue may affect their work hours. As the leader, you decide to open the store operating on a generator and provide work hours for employees who can safely travel to the store.

Not only will the decision you make ensure the employees can work to earn income, but the daily business operations will also continue as usual.

So you must assess organizational needs and decide how to proceed when unexpected situations occur.

3. Establish trust with employees

Good decision-making can help create a teamwork environment, as you can show employees that you value their work and best interests.

When a problem arises, everyone can discuss and determine different ways in which the problem can be solved. When you take the time to evaluate, analyze, and explain decisions, you also display thoughtfulness and trustworthiness. Employees will feel they can confide in you regarding their interests and concerns.

4. Reduce conflict

When you have decision-making as an option, you can help prevent fights, resolve misunderstandings, and improve concentration among employees in your workplace. This is because you'll set clear expectations for employees and provide direction on how your team can collaborate to achieve organizational goals.

By thinking from their perspective now and then, you can help them see things from yours. With this compatibility, you will remain motivated to practice more decision-making and apply it to all the problems in the workplace to promote shared understanding and less confusion.

Five Important Decision-Making Skills

As a leader who is also expected to be a decision-maker, you'll be responsible for evaluating risks and opportunities and staying committed to achieving the organization's goals.

So, I've put together five important skills you will need to make better decisions:

1. Research

Making an informed decision can be aided by gathering information through research. For instance, if you're a retail store manager and want to use social media to reach out to new customers, you can study the functions and users of various platforms. As a result, you are better equipped to select the most relevant platform that would appeal to your business's target market.

2. Creativity

You can create unique solutions to challenges using creativity. You can think about different solutions that might be more effective than a conventional one if you approach them with an open mind.

3. Critical thinking

You can leverage critical thinking abilities to weigh the advantages and disadvantages of the circumstance as you consider your options.

You can assess the potential advantages of one course and the dangers of another. To visualize the results of your decisions, you can apply visualization tools. Critical thinking abilities can also help you determine whether your team members can easily understand your company policies and whether your organizational goals are reasonable.

4. Time management

It's helpful to factor efficiency and scheduling into the decision-making process. Sometimes, investing extra time in analyzing and developing potential solutions hastens the conclusion of a decision. You can make decisions more quickly and effectively if you know how much time to allow for each task and where to focus your attention.

5. Emotional intelligence

When making decisions, it's critical to be conscious of and control your emotions. Being an engaged listener and empathizing while being impartial is especially crucial while participating in a group decision-making process. As you consider your options and offer your decision, try to be as concise and direct as possible. We will discuss emotional intelligence in more detail in the next section of this chapter and throughout Chapter 5.

GREAT LEADERS ARE GREAT DECISION-MAKERS

Decision-making is particularly important, considering its complex nature and the time it takes to make certain decisions.

Great leaders learn to balance emotion with reason to make decisions that positively impact their employees, customers, organization, and themselves. And because these judgments involve change, uncertainty, worry, tension, and, occasionally, the adverse reactions of others, making excellent decisions in challenging situations is no easy accomplishment.

You also need to know whether to move swiftly and use the knowledge at hand versus when to take your time and gather more information. You must also know when to stop should you pursue additional information or avenues. That's what great leaders do.

So in this section, we'll explore three crucial qualities you must develop to become a great leader who can make effective decisions.

Developing Emotional Intelligence

Emotional intelligence is the ability to identify, understand, and handle your emotions and those of others. It's another vital leadership quality every woman leader must possess. Your emotions are usually contagious as a leader, especially when you're a woman. Others will usually pick up on your mood, setting the tone for how people feel around you at work.

While emotional intelligence has several components, including self-management, self-awareness, social awareness, and relationship management, our focus here will be on self-management. And that's because once you understand the concept of self-management, you can get your emotions right.

Even when you feel strong emotions from others and yourself, you may still be aware of your emotions, be affected by them without being blinded, and calmly and effectively communicate your decisions to others.

Self-management is the capacity to understand and regulate your emotions, accommodate change, and cultivate an optimistic viewpoint.

Imagine yourself in a stressful, high-stakes situation where you have to decide what to do immediately. Your emotional response would probably be strong, and you might experience emotions like dread, rage, or anxiety.

Unfortunately, these emotions interfere with your capacity to make wise decisions. Usually, your first instinct will be to defend yourself as you enter the emotional section of your brain. Next, you experience an adrenaline rush or a flight-or-fight response, and your immediate priority is your short-term survival.

Being in this state is not ideal for developing long-term strategic judgments, which is why emotional restraint is crucial.

To become an exceptional leader, you must be aware of your emotional state and manage intense emotions to make intelligent decisions. You also need to learn how to calm the strong emotional response by using a different area of your brain (the prefrontal cortex)— which controls long-term planning and how we see the big picture—to make strategic, long-term judgments. Ironically, the best way to do this is to allow yourself to feel however you're feeling while consciously trying to keep your focus on the facts.

To try to stop feeling anything is like trying to prevent a roller coaster from going downhill. It takes so much work, but in the end, it backfires and makes you feel worse. Simply get on board and ride it out instead. The strength of the emotions will subside soon, allowing you to resume your rational thought process. However, removing emotions from the decision-making process is not the aim. It is merely to prevent them from seizing control and eroding emotional restraint.

As already mentioned in the previous section, we'll discuss emotional intelligence throughout Chapter 5, as it's a critical leadership skill you must develop.

Managing the Uncertainty of Choices

Have you ever wondered why making decisions is so difficult?

Perhaps it's because the variables and the outcomes are often uncertain.

It's human nature to dislike uncertainty, as discomfort and analysis paralysis result from it. So we consider the problem from all possible perspectives to reduce the feeling of ambiguity. But since you must make decisions very often amid uncertainty, these attempts are often fruitless and waste time and energy.

Therefore, before making judgments, why not think twice about your efforts to acquire certainty since you could be looking for a false sense of security?

Acceptance is an essential first step. You may concentrate your limited time, energy, and resources on choosing the best course of action during an uncertain decision if you accept the uncertainty rather than trying to resolve it. This doesn't imply you shouldn't consider things before choosing a course of action. Moreover, different analyses can give you the necessary knowledge to make the best decisions.

The secret is understanding when what you don't know is important and how to learn the information required to dispel the uncertainty. You should accept the uncertainty and proceed once you discover that what you don't know isn't important.

If you need help or devote too much time or other resources to the analyses, check if the uncertainty you are trying to address is indeed resolvable. It would be prudent to press forward despite the uncertainties if not.

In addition, you should make fewer options. Giving yourself many options is one of the blunders one makes while making decisions. You often believe you will make the best choice by carefully weighing your options. You may conduct this thorough search to eliminate doubt. You think that if you thoroughly investigate everything, nothing will be left to chance, and there will be no room for doubt. However, the issue is that you are prone to confusion and indecision.

You'll find it harder to decide when you have so many options. So limit your choices to make judgments more efficiently for you and your colleagues. It'll be simpler for you to decide if your options are limited to no more than five.

Trusting Your Intuition

Great leaders often follow their instincts when making decisions. They also claim they can stop being caught up in the loop of overthinking by having confidence in themselves and their knowledge.

Naturally, your intuition will be more trustworthy when you are familiar with a topic. Likewise, your finest guide will be your intuition if you become an authority in your profession.

So here's how to tune into your intuition:

You may have heard intuition defined as a persistent inner voice. Well, it sure is, so pay attention to it. Instead of shouting at you, it usually communicates softly. Unfortunately, ignoring your intuition in your constantly busy, technologically advanced environments is easy. Although our intuition continually speaks to us, we typically don't notice it.

Learn to trust your instincts; fortunately, practicing meditation daily can improve your ability to tune into your intuition. It doesn't have to be formal meditation; it could be a brief period of thought, a warm bath, a walk with your dog, etc. Simply schedule quiet times into your schedule, and you'll be astonished by how more sensitive you'll be to your intuition's voice.

In addition, building your self-confidence, as discussed in the previous chapter, and learning to follow your intuition will help you eliminate doubts and make the right decisions when facing different options. Meanwhile, remember not to be a perfectionist here and obsess about everything that may go wrong.

PRACTICING THE PROCESS

Like any other activity, top-notch decision-making takes practice. It's a procedure that calls for some tolerance for discomfort. We could play it safe and leave big decisions to others, agonize over every choice for hours on end, or accept the risk and move on.

Here are tips you can use to practice your decision-making skills, using all that we've discussed so far:

- Choose whether to act immediately or acquire more information. Create guidelines to help you decide what information is necessary and when to stop collecting information.

- As you move forward with your choice, be conscious of your emotions. Accept your feelings and let them lead you rather than rule you.
- Determine the degree to which the situation's uncertainty has to be resolved by recognizing its many components. Recognize that you cannot accurately predict most events and that it is usually essential to move forward despite discomfort.
- Listen to your intuition. Avoid second-guessing big choices because you can talk yourself into doing something that goes against your gut and past experiences.
- Look for opportunities to make complex decisions deliberately and proactively. Recognize that even "bad" results might be better than anticipated and develop faith in your capacity to make wise choices.

Many of us are concerned about making a wrong decision. However, we can only make the best decisions based on the information available. Usually, there is no right or wrong response. In the worst-case scenario, though, you decide against it. You will discover that you can manage the situation and make the best of it, even if the alternative you select turns out inferior in the short term. Going down the "wrong" route may even lead to unforeseen opportunities.

ESSENTIAL STRATEGIES TO IMPROVE YOUR DECISION-MAKING SKILLS

So far, I've been talking about how you can improve your decision-making skills. One thing that is worth bringing to your attention is that your decision-making capability will only improve if you make the most of your brain.

And to do so, you want to apply a combination of these essential strategies I've put together below. Some will directly improve your decision-making skills, and some will indirectly affect them. I recommend you practice each one daily to reap its full benefits.

Determine the benefits of the decision-making for you

Managing your self-interests, interpersonal relation-ships, and memories of past events and experiences are all aspects of indecision. To find out what's in it for you, first, recognize your feelings of attachment to the people involved. Name the memory that the current circumstance brings to mind. Finally, put safeguards in place with the help of a reliable partner, then build on what is evident.

Pay attention to your three "brains"

Surprised? Yes, we've got three brains, so use them. The cephalic (head) brain performs rational problem-solving, judgment, creativity, and empathy well. The heart (cardiac) brain is where passion, empathy, and values reside. Finally, the enteric (gut) brain stores courage, self-defense, and identity.

The three brains communicate with each other through the vagus nerve. Activating the vagus nerve benefits the heart and intestines, and Pranayama breathing exercises can help stimulate the vagus nerve. Pranayama is the name for breathing techniques that let our body's energy flow freely. We can remove physical and emotional obstacles in our bodies through deliberate breathing.

Fortunately, practicing Pranayama can lower high blood pressure too. People often report having more mental clarity and making better decisions after deep Pranayama breathing stimulates their vagus nerve. Similarly, vagus nerve stimulation is beneficial for the intestines. Over time, digestion becomes easier, and the gut functions better.

Adopting a regular breathing routine is an excellent option for practicing Pranayama. It doesn't need to be difficult in any way. Simply set aside ten minutes daily in a peaceful environment to focus inward and engage in the exercise. The lion's breath, belly breathing, and alternate nostril breathing are just a few techniques to explore. So try to find the method that works for you and make it part of your daily routine. Ultimately, the goal is to listen to all three brains and let them guide you in the decision-making process.

Identify the "who" and "why"

Making decisions about *who* is involved and *why* will improve your decision-making skill. A group decision can reveal viewpoints that can be voted upon if your choice impacts many individuals. A consultative choice can result in new perspectives if your judgment calls for the knowledge you need to gain. The last option is the autocratic decision, which is usually employed in dire situations or when you have the final say.

Take the 12-step approach

The 12-step approach is a battle-tested strategy to manage the unmanageable, find wisdom in acceptance, and show courage in the face of chaos. Here's what the 12-step approach looks like in making robust decisions:

THE 12-STEP APPROACH

01 MAXIMIZE PERSONAL DECISION-MAKING EFFECTIVENESS

The first step is the planning stage, which involves noting the likely decisions you'll have to make regarding the problem.

02 ENSURE TEAM AND ORGANIZATION EFFECTIVENESS

Before notifying your team about the problem, ensure they are up to the task of solving it. If not, then check what you can do to increase their effectiveness.

03 STATE THE PROBLEM

Once you're confident in your team's ability, inform the team about the specific work-related problem hindering the company's progress or productivity.

04 IDENTIFY THE CAUSE OF THE PROBLEM

After communicating the problem, the next step is brainstorming its possible causes so you can tackle them decisively.

05 LIST THE SOLUTIONS

Naturally, devising possible solutions becomes much easier once you identify the problem's specific causes.

06 DEFINE WHO THE SOLUTIONS WILL WORK FOR

It's also important to determine who the solutions will work for and how every team member can contribute to their success.

07 CHECK HOW EFFECTIVE THE SOLUTIONS ARE

You need to ensure the solutions are effective before acting on them. This will save you a lot of time, money, and other resources in the long term.

08 GENERATE ALTERNATIVE SOLUTIONS

Even if you decide the solutions are effective, it pays to have a backup plan in case things go wrong.

09 MEASURE YOUR KNOWLEDGE

Do you have the necessary knowledge to carry out these solutions? Are there opportunities for you to increase your knowledge? These are the questions you should continually ask yourself.

10 DETERMINE YOUR CONFIDENCE IN THE ALTERNATIVES ABILITY TO MEET YOUR GOALS

Measure the alternative solutions effectiveness as you did the main solutions.

11 DETERMINE YOUR OVERALL SATISFACTION WITH THE ALTERNATIVES

If the alternatives are satisfactory, move on to the next step. Otherwise, check what you can do to improve them.

12 DECIDE WHAT TO DO NEXT

Finally, now that you have an effective team and practical solutions, decide your next course of action. This could be delegating tasks, for instance.

The 12-step program instructs you to accept improvement rather than perfection. As you follow it, you'll discover that connection and gratitude are indeed superpowers.

Forget perfection

Everyone wants to choose the best course of action. But while there are both good and bad decisions, the ideal choice is uncommon. So put less emphasis on doing it perfectly and decide. Later, you can always change your mind. Put more focus on execution and buy-in.

Test the cost of not making a decision

It's easy to consider the benefits or drawbacks of deciding, but we often must remember to conduct a similar examination of doing nothing. With this extra analysis, you can determine the timing of a decision and the important turning point from a wait-and-see condition into a call to action. Your decision-making process is almost incomplete without this situational pressure testing.

Prioritize stakeholders

What should we do? This is usually our first question in even the most incompetent crisis response. That fosters a worldview that is self-referential and self-protective.

Instead, analyze your stakeholders and ask yourself, "What would responsible individuals among our stakeholders consider suitable for a responsible leader to do?"

For example, let's say your company's factory has direct and substantial implications on the environment and employees, while its supply chain impacts the environment, suppliers, and consumers.

What you want to do is identify your stakeholders and analyze how your decisions as a leader may help or impact them in regard to:

- The company's existing policies
- The lack of planning and design, best practices, and risks
- Evaluation of the implementation against initial assumptions

In the end, you'll see that prioritizing your stakeholders will help you make wiser decisions early.

Use the ten-point rule

Emotions play a significant role even when you believe you are making an objective decision. You should be more objective when using the rule of ten. Consider where it will take you after ten days, ten months, and ten years. Next, consider your reaction to the decision. It's also crucial to acknowledge and check in with your feelings.

Designate an antagonist

Make it a person's responsibility to provide compelling arguments to refute every decision you make. They can't make a decision better; their sole purpose is to reverse it. Imagine how much the person you choose learns about executive decision-making in that job. This third-party critique strategy is excellent for seeing things from multiple aspects, and it's a massive boost for them.

Recognize your formula

A formula, roadmap, or decision-making matrix is the surest strategy for making decisions as a leader. Putting processes and procedures into place creates a fence around your business when faced with a decision. When you use and adhere to these formulas for making decisions, indecision, the enemy of productivity, will be kept at bay.

Set goals and follow through with them

Clarifying their priorities and goals at the start of the year, every quarter, every month, and every week will help executives improve their decision-making abilities. It can help to have clear objectives and know when to communicate them in writing. Anyone who struggles with taking action has to practice just doing it.

Set a tight deadline

The longer you take to make a decision, the harder it is to make a decision, which may cause you to doubt your judgment. So be explicit about the time and date of the decision-making process and set a limited deadline. Also, use the time between collecting pertinent information to back up your choice. Usually, the more you do this, the easier and more natural it will be.

Consider your vision and values

Always refer to your organization's beliefs and vision while making a difficult choice. Your decisions should be filtered through and guided by these values. And know that you will err from time to time, but that is OK; just take something positive out of any mistake and learn from it.

Examine your biases

A crucial aspect of effective leadership is the ability to make decisions quickly. Yet sometimes, leaders tend to depend too heavily on their instincts, especially when time is of the essence and information is scarce. While using your instincts, you must also critically examine yourself and understand that "acting on your gut" sometimes means being influenced by your own biases.

Engage those who are qualified

After making complicated decisions, you may take a while to take action, so balance urgency and consideration. The most effective leaders understand how to involve appropriate parties in decision-making, but this doesn't mean you should consult everyone. Instead, it entails thinking carefully about whose viewpoint will improve the decision's quality.

Make a virtual board of directors

At any moment, but especially during a crisis, indecision is costly. Time is of the essence; uncertainty is considerable, and unexpected consequences could worsen matters. Through virtual decision support tools, executives may collaborate and systematically access the entire range of their trusted advisors. Make a virtual bulletin board of directors and explore alignment and divergent views.

You probably must have heard that great leaders lead by example, and indeed, they do. You've got to lead from the front to inspire others to change.

Once you can master the art of making good decisions, you'll be confident in yourself and others. And that leads us to another important subject we will cover in the next chapter—how to communicate your decisions correctly.

5

THE BEST COMMUNICATORS ARE THE BEST LEADERS

"Great communication begins with connection"

— OPRAH WINFREY

The content of a message consists of what is communicated. However, the verbal and nonverbal behavior that frames a message— the way that content is communicated—comprises one's communication style or the signals provided to help the process, interpret, filter, or understand the literal meaning.

How you communicate as a leader lends context to your message content. For example, just as two oral interpretations of the same poem may express that poem differently, different communication styles affect the perception of a message or set of messages.

As a leader, you are more than just a boss; you are responsible for communicating both the long-term and short-term vision and goals at every level. You show your colleagues their part in that vision and how they can all work together to get there.

Regardless of gender, effective communication is a fundamental leadership skill and a vital quality of a competent leader. Indeed, successful leadership and effective communication go hand in hand. So to inspire others to become achievers, a great leader must be a skilled communicator in many connections at the organizational level, in communities and groups, and, occasionally, on a worldwide scale.

You must be able to communicate your thoughts, reach out to various audiences, and share information. Additionally, you must manage the quick information flows across stakeholders, including consumers, partners, vendors, and other people you work with.

Just as leadership comprises different leadership techniques, communication consists of communication techniques, such as active listening, body language, negotiation skills, and the art of persuasion. The conscious and unconscious use of these techniques frames the content of a message. Over time, everyone develops a set of generally consistent behaviors that become their way of communicating.

THE SIGNIFICANCE OF COMMUNICATION

Communication can be more complex than the basic mechanics of sending and receiving information when it comes to leadership in business. When you harness the ability to communicate well as a leader, you'll be able to share information quickly and accurately.

One of the most fundamental qualities a woman leader can have is communication. To develop effective communication, you need direction and intention. You must also know when and how to communicate and choose the right channel for your target audience.

All forms of communication, including listening, body language, negotiating, and persuasion, require leaders to be excellent communicators. Only then can they meet their needs and build crucial interpersonal relationships.

Why Is Communication Important in Leadership?

The answer is straightforward—you cannot be a leader in isolation. That's right!

A hermit in a cave or a monk meditating on a mountaintop needs no leadership skills because they're all alone. However, your team will only implement your best idea for a new task if your communication is at least as intriguing as the idea itself.

To lead, you need to mobilize people. And to mobilize people, you need to build strong relationships with them. Likewise, you need the skills and ongoing commitment to communicating effectively with people.

Effective communication is crucial in every aspect of life; it can resolve merger pains, problem accounts, employee burnout, lawsuits, divorce, and even war. Communication is for leaders what water is for fish and air for birds. If you did nothing but live on a quest to be a great communicator, listener, and speaker, that quest would make you a great leader.

The good news is that virtually there is no issue we cannot resolve through communication. However, the bad news is that most of us command a small repertoire of communication skills. Usually, there is precious little specificity in our body language and almost none in how we listen to each other.

Important Facts about Communication

Before we examine specific distinctions of listening, body language, and negotiation, let's take a moment to look at these three essential facts about communication.

- **Authenticity counts:** Be sincere and truthful. Find your voice; refrain from speaking in corporate jargon or sounding vague. Your communication should reflect who you are, where you are, and what you value. Genuine leadership is what people want, respect, and will adhere to. So focus on being authentic instead of worrying about being eloquent. Don't try to hide your identity; people won't voluntarily follow someone they consider inauthentic.
- **Visibility is a form of communication:** Be approachable if you want to communicate effectively. Emails and official correspondence are insufficient, so be available, visible, and present. Consistently putting yourself out there demonstrates your leadership style to others. Often, people need to see and feel who you are to connect to the work you want them to accomplish. While communicating during a crisis, find ways to engage with all your stakeholder groups.
- **Listening is a powerful skill:** Good listeners also make good communicators. You may

clearly understand another's viewpoint and information when you listen well. Trust, respect, openness, and alignment are all fostered by listening. A crucial component of coaching others is active listening. Let folks express their worries. Ask compelling questions to gain access to people's innermost thoughts and emotions. Pay great attention to what is said and what is not described courteously.

As a leader, you cannot take communication with your team members for granted. Instead, you should take your words and that of other people seriously. When you take communication for granted, you pay a high price; you lose your ability to invent reality deliberately.

ACTIVE LISTENING

Active listening is when you give someone, say your employees or followers, your complete, undivided attention. Then, you listen attentively and focus entirely on your employees' words as they speak.

Active listening is one of the best-kept secrets of effective leadership. We learn very little when we speak because we usually say what we already know. But when we listen, we may learn something new while bestowing others the gift of our attention.

Paying close attention demonstrates respect for the speaker's words, ideas, sentiments, and emotions. When the person is done speaking, their self-esteem rises, and they feel more confident in their ability to speak up next time.

Take an organization with seven reporting levels, for instance. Let's say people at every level report 50% of what they know up to the next higher level, the leader at the top will know less than 2% of what is going on. If control resides solely at the top, the consequences of being that out of touch can be disastrous for decision-making. Imagine how this can negatively affect the organization if the leader bases their decisions on 98%+ of wrong information.

In today's complex and fast-changing organizations, managers and CEOs depend on vital strategic information from others, both within and outside the organization. And listening is a crucial vehicle for getting that strategic intelligence.

Below are some benefits of active listening:

- Improved communication throughout the organization

- Stronger relationships and trust among coworkers
- Greater confidence among employees
- Lower chance of work burnout
- Less conflict in the workplace
- Higher employee job satisfaction
- Higher rates of employee retention

Despite these fantastic benefits, listening remains an undervalued commodity. These days, nobody seems to listen anymore. Instead, talk abounds in our society. Day and night, we are inundated with infomercials and email broadcasts urging us to buy this or try that. Everyone has something to say.

Often, when people ask others to listen, they mean to say, "Shut up so I can talk." Listening is so invisible that it goes virtually unrecognized. Listening is noiseless; it's intangible and leaves little evidence. However, talk is loud and gets unnecessary attention.

Although listening is a fundamental skill, we're not usually taught how to do it. There are very few how-to books and virtually no schools on listening skills. Likewise, there are debating clubs and championships for orators but no showcases or awards for excellent listeners.

Active Listening Techniques

The following active listening techniques and skills will help you become a better active listener and leader:

- **Create a safe environment:** Creating a space where people feel comfortable talking about sensitive subjects is a fundamental active listening skill. Doing that might entail implementing an open communication policy that permits everyone to voice their ideas. As a leader, you may also maintain an open-door policy, inviting staff members to speak with you whenever needed.
- **Clear distractions:** It's impossible to listen attentively to someone and do anything else simultaneously. So take note of potential distractions and eliminate them. You could turn off your phone or leave your desk. But whatever you do, ensure the speaker has your full attention.
- **Ask questions and restate your words:** One of the best active listening techniques is to ask the speaker questions. Asking open-ended questions shows that you are paying attention and promotes continued conversation. Repeat some of what they've said to ensure you understand them.

- **Examine any nonverbal cues:** Don't just focus on what someone says verbally. Nonverbal communication can teach you much more about someone's thoughts, sentiments, and emotions. For instance, someone may sound confident yet project a lack of confidence through body language. You can usually find nonverbal cues in gestures, facial expressions, eye contact during conversation, and posture.

- **Recognize your emotions**: People may become emotional when discussing some subjects, especially sensitive ones or those involving private information. Recognize this and assure the other person that it's okay for them to feel these feelings. Don't be afraid to politely and respectfully ask them if they need a moment to gather their thoughts. Relationships at work are strengthened, and a sense of trust within the team is fostered by showing compassion and kindness in trying circumstances.

- **Establish eye contact:** One of the most important active listening techniques leaders need to master is maintaining precisely the appropriate amount of eye contact. If you do this continuously, the other person might feel uneasy and uncomfortable. Making little or no eye contact may give the impression that you are not listening. So find a polite compromise that demonstrates you are listening to all they say.

- **Do not interrupt:** Avoid interrupting others when they're speaking to you. Continuous interruptions are disrespectful and seem dismissive. It goes against listening in many ways and makes people reluctant to talk to you about anything.

- **Know when to change the topic**: Knowing when to switch topics is one of the most underutilized active listening strategies. Before changing the subject, confirm that the communication has ended. Ask the person if they have any other comments. Changing topics and discussing something else is appropriate once you've covered all the necessary points. Too much will be left unsaid if you switch topics too soon, and people can become irritated.

- **Smile appropriately:** If you smile too often during a sensitive conversation, it could look weird. And people could interpret your lack of action as cold body language. In addition, others may be reluctant to approach you or express an honest view. So, only smile when it is proper to do so. Otherwise, it could send the wrong message.

- **Make it a discussion:** Most people listen to respond rather than to understand. Seeking understanding entails engaging in genuine dialogue. You're not listening to someone if all you want to do is have your turn to talk. Being attentive to what they're saying requires the give-and-take of a genuine discussion in which both parties get something from the exchange.

- **Follow good examples:** Find someone who has mastered a skill you wish to learn, then imitate their behavior. Consider some leaders who are excellent models of active listening. The next time you speak with them, pay attention to how they use active listening. What do you observe about their communication style? What methods of active listening do they employ that you should practice? These questions can help you identify your areas for development.

Listening takes sustained effort to develop but yields surprising results to those who dare to make it a life-long quest. As a leader, you can make or break people around you by the way you listen to them. But just as listening to others can encourage and enable them, not listening can damage a person's spirit and effectiveness.

BODY LANGUAGE

Did you realize that you have a natural advantage that you may use in critical professional circumstances like job interviews, negotiations, presentations, and so on?

Oh, yea! It's right there, waiting for you to grasp it and use it as a potent yet undetectable key to success.

And it's your body language.

Body language, also known as nonverbal communication, is a fascinating subject. Establishing fruitful business connections, connecting with team members, making presentations with the most impact, and projecting a sense of leadership presence are essential.

Knowing your body language can alter the course of a business conversation for the better or worse is crucial. For instance, instead of turning your glance from a male colleague's eyes to his mouth, you change your gaze into one more appropriate for social situations. A social gaze can be seen as flirting, even in a professional setting. You need to be aware of your body language and learn to leverage it.

The following are some nonverbal cues you should be mindful of:

1. Head tilts

In the past, tilting the head helped people hear sounds of danger more clearly and take decisive action. Today, tilting one's head can indicate interest and personal involvement, especially with women.

Although head tilts can serve as helpful indications, they are also unconsciously interpreted as signals of submission. So keep your head straight and neutral, especially when conducting business with men.

2. Handshake

Women who shake hands firmly leave a better first impression and are more often perceived as confident.

Spend some time perfecting your business handshake. Keep your body facing the other person fully and squared off to them. Aim for palm-to-palm contact and make sure the other person's web of the hand (the skin between the thumb and first finger) meets your web. Above all, shake hands firmly.

3. Vocal pitch

Women usually raise their voices at the end of phrases as if asking a question or looking for affirmation.

Instead, use the authoritative arc, in which your voice begins on one note, climbs in pitch throughout the sentence, and then falls back down at the conclusion whenever you make a definite assertion.

4. Smiling

Smiling too much or in improper situations can make you less likable and less trustworthy, especially if you do this when discussing a delicate subject.

Smiling can be one of the most significant and pleasant nonverbal signs when used appropriately, such as during an initial encounter with a potential business client. It is highly effective at conveying friendliness and likeability. However, you must appear serious when the conversation becomes serious.

5. Head nods

We usually nod when we agree with something or someone. Nodding is a sign of agreement or that you are paying attention, empathizing with, or supporting the speaker. The constant nodding of the head can convey involvement and encouragement but not authority or power. Keep your head still to convey confidence, especially when expressing your views.

6. Expressing emotion

Women who show their emotions with hand gestures that rise over their shoulders may seem erratic, even though a certain degree of energy can add passion and substance to a message.

A presentation that is emotionally engaging and motivating can be tremendously powerful. But when you want to exert as much authority as possible, it's best to keep your movements to a minimum and show composure under pressure.

7. Space

Women often project their bodies in a way that makes them appear less competent, less like a leader, with their elbows kept close to their sides and their knees tightly crossed.

Keep in mind that height and distance serve to amplify a leader's presence without using words. So look like the extraordinary leader you are by standing or sitting tall, pulling your shoulders back, widening your stance, moving your arms away from your torso, and holding your head high.

Becoming more conscious of your posture, voice, gaze, and other nonverbal clues is only one part of the solution. The capacity to decipher other people's body language makes up the other half. And this is where being a woman truly works in your favor.

Women are better at reading nonverbal clues and more tuned to relationship dynamics. You'll agree that how our intuition has developed into a genuine and potent leadership skill is fascinating.

NEGOTIATION SKILLS

Negotiation skills enable two or more parties to come to an agreement. Soft skills like communication, emotional intelligence, planning, strategizing, and persuasion are usually a part of this list. Although negotiation skills are situational or contextual, ideally, the first step to becoming a better negotiator is to understand these skills. And we'll explore some of them shortly.

Early in 2008, Sheryl Sandberg, former vice president of global sales and operations at Google, came under Mark Zuckerberg's consideration for the role of the chief operating officer at Facebook. The two met for almost two months to discuss Facebook's goals and future.

Finally, Zuckerberg presented a proposal. According to Sandberg, in her book *Lean In: Women, Work, and the Will to Lead*, she thought it was fair and was anxious to accept the position, but her husband persuaded her not to take the first offer on the table.

Sandberg hesitated out of concern for Zuckerberg's feelings. Sheryl was about to accept when her brother-in-law said, "Damn it, Sheryl! Why are you going to work for less money than any male would make from the same job?"

Sandberg acknowledged that he was right. She reminded Zuckerberg that she was being hired to lead his deal teams and that he should anticipate aggressive negotiating from her. She set out what she wanted and stated, "This is the only time you and I will ever be on opposing sides of the table."

And the result?

Zuckerberg gave her a far greater offer the following day. Sandberg's type of negotiation skill is called "principled negotiation." Every aspect of life recognizes the value of negotiation skills, but you need them more in business and the workplace. Below are the different types of negotiation skills:

- **Principled negotiation:** This is a negotiation style where you solve an issue by balancing the interests and principles of both parties. Conflict resolution is frequently the main focus of this kind of negotiation. This form of negotiation employs an integrative negotiation strategy to advance the interests of both parties.

- **Team negotiation:** Multiple persons negotiate on both sides in a team negotiation. You'll find yourself doing team negotiations with large business deals.

- **Multiparty negotiation:** This is a negotiation involving more than two parties. Bargaining between various department heads of a large company exemplifies a multiparty negotiation.

Mastering negotiation techniques is even more crucial if you hold high-profile roles such as executive, sales manager, or other top leadership positions. Negotiating effectively can mean the difference between winning or losing a business.

The Rules of Negotiation and How to Get Better at It

Although many other negotiation strategies are available, I want to share the six main guidelines for improving your negotiating skills. Knowing these guidelines will enable you to appreciate the significance of negotiation in leadership.

- **First, put yourself in their shoes:** To find ways to avoid conflict, especially deep-seated conflicts, and reach an agreement with adversaries, Madeleine Albright, former U.S. secretary of state, recommends close observation and perspective taking. Albright believes the key to successful negotiation is finding out as much as possible from the other person and understanding their needs.

- **Be open-minded:** It's essential to maintain an open mind during negotiations and to stay free of ego and bias. Ultimately, it comes down to controlling your emotions throughout the negotiation process. You can improve commercial relationships by keeping your feelings upbeat. Negotiations, problem-solving, and decision-making become more straightforward as a result.

- **Timing is essential:** Negotiations ought to have a deadline. It is equally important to know what to ask for and when to ask for it. You need to know when to move ahead and stand back in negotiations if you want to be successful. When everything falls into place as anticipated and planned, it's time to push and obtain what you came for. However, avoid rushing or pushing yourself too far, as this can negatively impact business relations.

- **Active listening:** Successful negotiators actively listen to the opposing party while understanding their body language. Finding areas of shared interest and determining whether your counterpart will accept or reject your suggestion depend heavily on active listening.

- **Keep your word:** The agreements between parties impact the negotiation's conclusion, and both sides risk losing their integrity if they don't keep their promises. Trust is one of those things that is almost impossible to regain once lost. As a result, future discussions will be unsuccessful, and the other person might refuse to do business with you. If you want to negotiate successfully, make only agreements you can keep.

- **Have alternatives:** It's usually a good idea to have high standards. Realistic thinking about things is also a good idea. But what happens if the initial strategy fails to secure a deal? Do you have any alternatives? If not, begin addressing them as you prepare for your next conversations. This will enable you to be more adaptable and cooperative as necessary.

As you can see, bargaining and leadership are complementary skills. The procedure itself has several applications. You may succeed in negotiations by developing a solid plan, and how you prepare for discussions will determine your success. The success of your negotiations as a skilled negotiator depends on your capacity to consider every important factor. You must locate and evaluate each option. Be realistic and avoid bias as well.

THE ART OF PERSUASION

Your opportunity to use persuasion skills dramatically increases as you form healthy relationships.

Similar to sales or manipulation, the word "persuasion" can get a bad reputation in the workplace. But I believe every woman needs this vital skill to succeed as a leader.

Your ability to persuade others provides you with the ability to

- advocate for more responsibility;
- encourage your staff to take action;
- convince potential investors to fund your business;
- get a raise or a promotion; and

- convince a potential client to hire you.

One of the most crucial abilities for women in the workplace may be persuasion—the ability to persuade others can advance your ideas, profession, or yourself. Among other benefits, this can help you continue your ascent to the top.

The Formula for Being Persuasive

If you want to become persuasive but aren't there as yet, I've got good news for you. Indeed, you can develop your persuasive skills using the formula I've outlined below:

- **Ethos or "character":** Ethos is the section of a speech or presentation where your audience begins to believe you are credible. And credibility is vital as a base for persuasion.
- **Logos or "reason":** You are developing a rational case for why your audience should be interested in your argument or proposal using data, evidence, and facts. No matter how strong your facts or evidence is, if your audience doesn't care, you won't succeed.
- **Pathos or "emotion":** People are motivated to take action by a speaker's emotional impact. Although being open and vulnerable can be

frightening, it's often the quickest method to establish the connection that inspires action.

- **Metaphor:** Using a metaphor or comparison to link a novel idea to something well known to your audience helps clarify your point by making the abstract concrete. For example, let's say you're trying to tell a novice about the function of an automobile. You can say, "It's a carriage that moves without a horse—a horseless carriage." That way, the person will clearly understand what an automobile does without much talking.

- **Brevity:** The amount of knowledge the human brain can absorb and retain has fairly universal upper and lower bounds. Therefore, you should preserve succinctness and begin with your strongest argument. For example, if you're having a meeting, I recommend you start with the most vital three of all your points, as studies have proven three to be the best number for retention. Afterward, you can proceed to discuss the following two points. Keep things short to enable your audience to digest your message efficiently and remember them long after they've left the meeting.

Tips for Business Women to Help Fine-Tune Persuasion Skills

Furthermore, below I have shared additional tips you can use to refine your persuasion powers:

- **Use empathy:** Empathy is a trait that women naturally possess, which helps hone persuasion skills. You can use it to read other people's reactions and then apply that knowledge in a way that speaks to your listeners' worries.
- **Use names often:** Use names often because people will respond when you call them by name. So learn their names as soon as possible and use them when working with others. It will boost their egos, which will lead to stronger connections. With established relationships, you can easily convince people in this manner.
- **Use reciprocity:** When someone does something for us, we often feel bound to return the favor. This idea serves as the basis for persuasion in business. Precise reciprocity techniques include sales, coupons, and special promotions. Therefore, if you give people anything—information, freebies, or a satisfying experience—they will want to return the favor. This could be in the form of a great review or referral.

- **Use images:** Often, what we see and do not hear is much more significant. Because of this reality, you must know what your team members, clients, and consumers see. So create a professional first impression using images that convey a narrative. You can control emotional responses and improve your persuasion skills by doing so.
- **Use undisputed facts:** Establish trust by starting conversations with an obvious fact. By doing this, you are giving your client a factual statement that they may accept. Likewise, when you start with a topic you both agree on, you establish trust with them immediately. Undisputed facts lead to additional agreements, which makes persuading a client to adopt your point of view simpler.
- **Leverage social proof:** When people aren't sure what to do, they turn to others for direction. They are curious about what other people are choosing or doing. As a result, you can effectively employ peer pressure to influence their decisions when you use social proof. Peer pressure is something we never truly get over. Ideally, testimonials from pleased customers will show your target market that others like them liked your offering.

OTHER SUGGESTIONS FOR IMPROVEMENT

Here are some strategies to enhance your leadership communication abilities, whether for a presentation to your company's board of directors, landing a new client, or running a regular staff meeting:

- **Be present:** When you check your phone or other devices while someone else is talking, people will notice and are less likely to give you their full attention when it's your turn to speak. So remove any distractions from meetings and pay attention to what others say.
- **Know your audience:** Create your messages with your target audience in mind. Are they seasoned professionals or newcomers? Are you trying to convince a customer or improve your relations with your team? Use the method of communication they prefer.
- **Focus on the purpose of your communication and be succinct:** Prioritize your goals for every interaction. Make sure interactions are on-topic; keep your messages brief and concentrate on this goal.
- **Never stop learning:** Effective leaders value self-improvement and lifelong learning. You and your team can gain the competitive edge

they need by pursuing professional development in crucial areas like effective communication.

- **Be your greatest advocate:** Negative self-image can still slow your progress. Avoid second-guessing yourself and thinking if you are acting too aggressively. Think highly of yourself and become your greatest advocate.

- **Become unapologetically visible:** Leaders use both verbal and nonverbal communication. Standing up while speaking will make women in leadership positions seem more confident and overcome a softer voice.

- **Connect with others:** Learn how to communicate effectively with others. Also, always project confidence when in the workplace. You can use phone or video calls to establish human contact when working remotely. But always use first names to address your coworkers and staff and be sure to ask them about their concerns and what matters to them.

- **Know your value and express it:** Be aware of what lends you credibility, and don't be afraid to mention it. This could be your credentials, experience, or performance. If feasible, establish credibility early on in the connection, whether through a casual discussion or a formal presentation. You should always articulate what makes you credible.

- **Relax:** Collaboration is key in today's corporate world. Leaders can inspire people to work as a team and achieve goals. This requires effort, trust, and communication. Therefore, make time to unwind and recharge when you're working hard. Know what you can and can't control. In doing so, you'll be present with others and the current situation, increasing your awareness of what you need to maintain momentum.

So much of what we think of "leading" and "leadership" depends on or simply is some variety of communication activity or process. Leadership fundamentally involves influence; the ability to influence requires power and influencing processes and perceptions of power depend on communication.

Also, a critical resource of leaders is vision, along with the ability to encourage and integrate individual ideas into a compelling shared vision. Leaders' visions include symbols, images, languages, and symbolic actions. Visions are made up of communication.

Leadership is almost entirely a communication activity, more so than any other activity. There's another skill through which you can learn empathy to communicate and better relate with others: emotional intelligence.

Emotional intelligence enhances the ability to weigh words and mannerisms and to ensure they are the right fit for a situation. Good leaders must be caring, empathetic, supportive, and considerate and give personalized attention to those around them. These character traits may be more accessible for an individual with high emotional intelligence.

Thus, our discussion in the next chapter is on emotional intelligence. Internalizing its importance and applying it well yields positive leadership results. Emotional intelligence is indeed a vital tool for leaders in today's dynamic world.

AN EASY WAY TO PULL OTHER WOMEN UP WITH YOU

"The more women help one another, the more we help ourselves. Acting like a coalition truly does produce results."

— SHERYL SANDBERG

Sheryl Sandberg, former COO of Meta Platforms, is a role model for female leaders everywhere... and she's right. We're operating in a world built for men, and as we pull other women up the ladder with us, we create a world in which gender equity grows ever closer.

A successful leader lights the path for her team, showing support and inspiring those around her... and that can have ramifications not just for her organization, but for the world around her too.

As you gain confidence in your skills as a leader and integrate the new techniques you're learning into your practice, you have a chance to pull other female leaders up with you – and doing that is easier than you think.

It's in the little things – it's in sharing your knowledge and experience with others; it's in offering support to those who are struggling; it's in networking and helping others to forge valuable connections. It's even in leaving a short book review.

Let me explain... By taking just a few minutes to leave your honest feedback on this book, you'll help other women like you find the guidance they're looking for.

By leaving a review of this book on Amazon, you'll light the path for other female leaders looking to expand their skills and adopt new techniques.

It's these little acts that allow us to make a difference to each other... and best of all, they barely eat into our already bursting schedules.

Simply by letting other readers know how this book has helped you and what they will find within its pages, you'll help bring other women up the ladder with you. Thank you for your support. It's tough being a woman in leadership... but together, we have incredible power.

Scan the QR code below to leave a quick review!

6

LEVEL UP YOUR EQ (EMOTIONAL INTELLIGENCE)

"I've learned that people will forget what you said, people will forget what you did, but people will never forget how you made them feel."

— MAYA ANGELOU

Almost every five-year-old laughs when playing with their pet and cries when their parents tell them they've eaten enough sweet pastries for a day. Now, imagine you meet a five-year-old girl like this named Trisha. Unlike most five-year-olds, Trisha speaks three languages fluently, which you'll agree is impressive. Better yet, she never took a course or worked too hard at learning the three languages.

Now, let's say as an adult, you don't speak three languages fluently. Does that mean Trisha is smarter than you? And does it mean her brain is more capable than yours, even at age five?

No, it doesn't! Yet, Trisha is more capable than you are at speaking three languages. But that's because she was more exposed to languages than you were.

But even though Trisha has foreign language skills you lack, if you choose, you could acquire the same degree of proficiency. This is true for anyone who decides to study a foreign language and consistently practices becoming better at communication.

Mastering the language of emotional intelligence is no different. We all can learn it, but our capacity to do this remains dormant until we become aware of it and recognize the value of acquiring it.

When we observe a leader skilled at connecting with others and bringing out the best in them, we become conscious of "people skills," though we might not know how to acquire those skills.

However, since we can learn foreign languages, we can expand our emotional literacy and improve our leadership skills through focused study and determination. Once you drop the assumption that someone is naturally more brilliant or innately gifted, you can get down to learning.

It's easy for most of us to identify the people who have brought out the best in us, and it's even easier to remember those who have brought out the worst. Because of how these managers made us feel, these memories are important. And this supports Maya Angelou's quote, which I shared at the beginning of the chapter.

Every interaction, whether in business or at the office, is influenced by our emotions. They affect how we respond to opportunities and difficulties. They also determine whether we work together to overcome disputes. In addition, they increase our capacity to forgive ourselves and those who offend us.

A female boss who has developed her emotional intelligence finds it easy to trust, respect, and display positivity among her colleagues. Employees want to be valued and respected in the workplace by management. And if you can build empathy, you will thrive easily.

Our emotions affect how much effort we put out, our behaviors, our psychological health, and our moods as we go about our daily lives. That is why there is a strong correlation between emotional intelligence and good leadership. And so, in this chapter, you'll explore what emotional intelligence is and why it's an essential trait for a woman leader.

EMOTIONAL INTELLIGENCE AND LEADERSHIP EFFECTIVENESS

Daniel Goleman's *Emotional Intelligence: Why It Can Matter More Than IQ*, published in 1995, lends prominence to emotional intelligence as a field of psychology. Today, emotional intelligence is a widely applied model for understanding how people can manage emotions, empathize with other people's feelings, and enhance their relationships.

Emotional intelligence deals with our capacity to acknowledge, understand, and deal with our emotions and those of others. Also known as emotional quotient (EQ), emotional intelligence is more valuable than intellect, as it helps us manage relationships intelligently and compassionately as leaders.

Importance of Emotional Intelligence for Leaders

You may wonder why you should spend time and effort improving your EQ. The simple answer is that leaders shape the culture of their company. So a lack of emotional intelligence could have more severe repercussions, such as reduced employee engagement and morale.

However, a higher emotional intelligence deepens self-knowledge and improves relationships, whether those relationships are with people in business or your personal life. In essence, having a high EQ as a leader translates to greater employee engagement.

Effective leadership requires developing emotional connections with others and leading with emotional intelligence. That's partly because how a leader makes you feel can affect your engagement and productivity. Every job environment you encounter can involve emotions, including the following:

- Change and uncertainty
- Interactions between coworkers
- Relations and conflict
- Burnout and effort
- Success and failure

Usually, the managers with the most significant impact on one's job satisfaction have high levels of emotional intelligence and leadership efficiency. In addition, they bring out the best in their workers because they are strong communicators and empathetic, making their employees feel appreciated.

Key Components of Emotional Intelligence

According to Goleman, there are five key components of emotional intelligence. The more you understand how to manage each of these elements of emotional intelligence, the easier it will be to achieve personal happiness and professional success. So, let's look at each component in detail and examine how you can use them to grow as a leader.

- **Self-awareness:** You are always aware of how you feel and how your actions and feelings may affect those around you. As a leader, self-awareness entails acting with humility and clearly understanding your talents and flaws.
- **Self-control:** Leaders who control their emotions are less likely to verbally attack others, act rashly or emotionally, stereotype others, or violate their moral principles. The main goal of self-regulation is maintaining control. According to Goleman, this aspect of emotional intelligence also includes a leader's flexibility and dedication to personal accountability.
- **Motivation:** Self-motivated leaders continually work toward their objectives and hold themselves to very high standards for the caliber of their work.

- **Empathy:** Empathy is essential for managers of successful teams or organizations. Empathetic leaders can imagine themselves in other people's shoes. They also support team members' growth, confront unjust behavior in others, offer constructive criticism, and show empathy for those in need. Showing your colleagues you care by being empathic will help you win their respect and loyalty.
- **Social skills:** Leaders who excel in this component of emotional intelligence are excellent communicators. They are adept at rallying their team behind them and getting them excited about a new mission or project; they are equally receptive to receiving both good and bad news. Furthermore, leaders with strong interpersonal skills are adept at handling disagreements and implementing change. They rarely accept things as they are; they also don't just sit back and let others take everything. Instead, they lead by example.

In the subsequent sections of this chapter, you'll learn how to build and improve your EQ to help you become a successful leader.

They Are Judging You on Emotions

According to recent research, how leaders show their emotions significantly affects how others see them. Thomas Sy, a psychology professor at UC Riverside, and Daan van Knippenberg, a management professor at Drexel University, studied how a leader's emotional displays influence people's perceptions of their effectiveness.

The study's six emotional leadership schemas—joy, calm, pride, anger, fear, and remorse—were divided into three positive and two negative categories. The ideas of the emotional qualities and actions that distinguish leaders are what the authors refer to as these schemas or Implicit Theories of Leadership Emotions (ITLEs).

Sy and van Knippenberg's work is based on the Implicit Leadership Theory (ILT), a well-researched idea that claims people have implicit expectations and preconceptions about the characteristics that constitute excellent leadership.

The higher the organizational structure you go, the more apparent ITLEs are (or the emotional "schemas" people use to determine whether or not a leader is effective).

People can assess a leader's efficacy when they routinely contact them, such as their immediate boss or supervisor. But they typically don't interact with or learn much about those in positions of authority. As a result, they frequently rely on schemas. And schemas are effective, as they influence our behavior even without data.

The new study also demonstrates that people have expectations regarding the emotions good leaders portray and that women leaders are subject to different evaluations because they consistently battle old, sexist preconceptions.

It also shows that because women still believe they must dispel the myth that they are "too emotional" to be great leaders, women leaders tend to display fewer negative emotions than their male counterparts. Compared to male leaders, female leaders generated higher levels of cheer and lower levels of fear, anger, and remorse.

Another 2016 study found that female leaders can suffer consequences for even mild or moderate displays of emotion, mainly when the emotion implies authority, such as rage or pride. However, being emotionally inactive can also have negative consequences because it's believed that emotionally flat women don't meet their warm, social obligations as women.

This study highlights the gender stereotypes that women are still working to dispel and the necessity of emotional intelligence at all levels of leadership.

Everyone, regardless of gender, has good and bad feelings, and a lack of emotional expression can also harm how others view a leader. For instance, emotionless and robotic leaders may find it challenging to inspire their staff members.

Different emotional reactions are also required in some circumstances. For instance, a CEO expressing regret after a significant mishap their employees caused would be appropriate and indicative of excellent leadership, even if regret is a negative feeling.

Emotional intelligence is key, which allows you to make emotions work for you but not against you.

EMOTIONAL INTELLIGENCE IS YOUR SECRET WEAPON

I've always had a strong voice, but I've never had a loud one.

When men or women confuse these two voices, it can cause a lot of confusion. Many business owners, entrepreneurs, and leaders have historically been men who rose to the top by intimidation and force. Many females are experimenting with the same approach to see where it can lead them.

Unfortunately, women still struggle to obtain and maintain positions at the highest levels of authority, despite dying from heart disease at a rate equal to that of men.

I had a choice in my career: I could pretend to be someone I'm not and strut around the managers' meetings. Or I could be the best version of myself by honing my people skills and letting go of concerns about whether or not I belonged with others who led with intimidation.

Here are three reasons why, as a woman leader, emotional intelligence can be your secret weapon:

1. Women are likelier to be emotionally intelligent than men

Women need to succeed however they can, but too many are wasting their advantages by acting like males.

Society gives young females the go-ahead to practice empathy, use language that conveys feelings, and prioritize long-lasting constructive connections (starting with dolls and dollhouses).

While playing sports can help girls and boys become mentally robust, many boys grow up to be men who react to stress by using more arduous abilities like violence rather than softer ones like empathy and self-awareness.

On the other hand, women are urged to acquire these soft skills, and the good news is that you may do so as you advance in your profession.

2. Women executives rank highest in emotional intelligence

High levels of emotional intelligence were discovered in work settings where female executives were obliged to lead by influence rather than direct authority, according to an intriguing study by the Hay Group.

In this study, women executive-level employees exhibited more vital emotional intelligence skills than men. It is thought that difficulties women encounter throughout their professions force them to acquire the emotional intelligence abilities necessary to advance in their organizations.

3. Women's brains are different

Women are said to have greater empathy. According to neuroscientists, empathy is located in the insula, a part of the brain that receives messages from all over our body. The insula reads the pattern our brains create when empathizing with someone and recognizing the feeling.

Women differ from men in this area. For instance, women's brains tend to stick with the other person's emotions when upset. However, men's brains act differently. After briefly registering another's feelings, they tune them out and shift their attention to other brain regions that work to address the issue causing the disturbance.

Therefore, when a woman claims that a man is emotionally disconnected, it is probably due to the differences in how our brains receive information. Men who tune out can shield themselves from stress and remain composed, while others are engrossed in high drama. They concentrate on solving the pressing issue. In contrast, women's propensity to pay attention makes it easier for them to care for and assist others when their emotions are intense.

As a woman leader, you need to improve your emotional intelligence because it increases your capacity to handle pressure, establish trust, bargain, persuade, deal with office politics, and take calculated risks. Regardless of your age, you can always work to build your emotional intelligence.

Managing Your Emotions at Work

How can you manage your emotions better and "choose" how you respond to challenging circumstances? That's precisely what we want to discuss here, so let's look into the most common negative emotions women experience in the workplace.

If you are wondering why we focus only on negative emotions, that's because most of us don't need a guide to manage our positive emotions. After all, positive emotions like happiness, excitement, compassion, or optimism hardly ever hurt other people. Furthermore, positive emotions are great at work as long as they are expressed productively and professionally. So let's discuss how you can manage your negative emotions effectively.

1. Frustration and irritation

Generally, frustration happens when you feel unable to move forward, confined, or stuck in another way. This could be a coworker obstructing your preferred project, a client too disorganized to arrive at your meeting on time, or even someone putting you on hold for too long.

Whatever the source, it's critical to deal with feelings of frustration as soon as possible since they can quickly turn into more unpleasant emotions, including anger.

Here are ways to deal with frustration:

- **Stop and evaluate:** You should pause your thoughts and assess the situation; ask yourself what could have gone wrong. Put it in writing and be specific, then consider one advantage of your current circumstance. For instance, you will have extra time to prepare if a client is late for the meeting. Or you could take a moment to unwind.
- **Identify a particular benefit in the situation:** It usually helps to focus on a positive aspect of your situation to change how you perceive it. This minor shift in perspective can lift your spirits. For instance, when other people are the source of your irritation, they may not be doing it on purpose. So try not to be angry; instead, carry on with your activities.

When was the last time you got irritated? If you think hard enough, you'll see that whatever upsets you usually get resolved after some time. You might also realize your displeasure or annoyance didn't help much to resolve the issue back then, so it likely won't help you today, either.

2. Worry and nervousness

Understandably, many people worry about their careers, given all the dread and anxiety of increased layoffs. However, if you allow it, this worry may quickly spiral out of hand, harming your mental health, productivity, and willingness to take risks.

Try these tips to deal with worrying:

- **Avoid being surrounded by anxiety and worry:** For instance, if coworkers are chatting about layoffs in the break room, resist the urge to join them in their fear. Nobody benefits from worrying since worrying often results in more worrying.
- **Try practicing deep breathing:** Deep breaths lower your heart and breathing rates. So take a five-second deep breath in, followed by a five-second deep breath out. You should pay attention to only your breathing during each session. Repeat this at least five times.
- **Think about improving things:** You can't keep your job if you sit and worry about getting fired. Instead of giving in to fear, why not develop creative strategies to increase sales and prove your worth to the company?

- **Create a concern log and list your problems there:** If you discover that worries are circling in your head, write them down in a journal or "worry log," then set aside time to address them. You may put these concerns to rest until then. Conduct a thorough risk analysis of these circumstances regarding the time you've allotted to them, then take the appropriate steps to reduce any risks.

Your confidence can suffer if you're anxious and concerned about anything. So you want to prevent this from happening. Also, you shouldn't allow your worries to get in your way of being appropriately assertive.

3. Anger and aggravation

When out of control, people's most damaging emotion at work is rage. Additionally, it's an emotion that most of us have trouble managing. One of the best things you can do to keep your job is to learn to control your temper if you have difficulties doing so at work.

To manage your anger, consider the following ideas:

- **Watch out for early signs of anger:** Learn to spot the warning signals when anger grows because only you will know when they appear. Early control of your anger is essential;

remember, you can choose how you respond to events. Just because becoming upset is your initial impulse doesn't mean it's the best course of action.

- **Stop what you're doing if you feel angry:** Practice the deep breathing technique we previously discussed while closing your eyes. This cuts off your angry thoughts and helps you get back on the right track.

Imagine yourself in a furious state: You can gain some perspective on the situation if you picture how you might appear and act in an angry state. For example, consider how you would look if you were about to yell at a coworker. Is your face rosy? Do you have your arms raised? Would you like to work with anyone like that? Most likely not. The same goes for your colleagues and employees.

4. Dislike

Most likely, we've all had to work with people we don't like. However, it's imperative to maintain professionalism at all times.

Here are some ideas for working with people you dislike:

- **Be respectful:** It's time to put your pride and ego aside if you work with someone you dislike. So be courteous and respectful to the person as you would to anyone else. You shouldn't act in a similarly unprofessional manner just because this person does.
- **Be assertive:** If the other person is being unprofessional and disrespectful, firmly state that you will not tolerate such behavior, then calmly leave the situation. If you have to take further disciplinary actions, then do so. Always lead by example.

5. Disappointment and unhappiness

It might be challenging to deal with disappointment or unhappiness at work. These feelings are the most likely to affect your productivity at work of all the emotions you could experience. After a significant setback, your energy will likely be low, and you might be hesitant to take risks, which could prevent you from accomplishing.

You can take the following proactive measures to deal with disappointment and unhappiness:

- **Examine your mindset:** Take time to examine your attitude and accept that not everything will go your way. Wouldn't life be a straight route without ups and downs, hills and valleys if it did? The hills and valleys are what usually add spice to life.
- **Adjust your aim:** Just because you were unhappy you didn't achieve a goal doesn't mean it's still impossible. Maintain the objective but make minor adjustments, such as delaying the deadline.
- **Write down your thoughts:** List the reasons you're dissatisfied with your work. Is it a colleague? Is it the pressure? Once you identify the issue, begin formulating solutions or workarounds. Always keep in mind that you can improve your situation.
- **Smile:** Even though it may seem unusual, wearing a smile or even a grimace can make you feel happier; this is one of the strange ways humans are wired. So always smile!

Great Leaders Have Emotional Control

Emotional control is a skill you must have as a leader to manage your employees successfully. In times of upheaval and change, workers frequently seek leaders for guidance on how to act. As a result, you must prepare to wear a composed, logical look as a leader. In addition, leaders are viewed as more pleasant, moral, and dedicated to the organization when they have strong emotional control. Here's how to improve your emotional control:

1. Understand the value of emotions

Suppressing feelings is not the same as controlling them. Emotions may significantly impact a business, and you need to be aware of this. You can apply emotions to frame recent occurrences or circumstances positively. For instance, you can show confidence in someone by acting positively toward them.

According to research, managers who severely repress their feelings are less content with their jobs, more likely to desire to leave their companies, and may have a detrimental effect on the work of their direct reports. Likewise, it's possible to display less positive emotions under stress or pressure. These feelings could include worry, annoyance, frustration, or fury. This is why you must be cautious about this.

Employees may become alarmed if they experience extreme anxiety, tension, or distraction when the organization is transitioning. The likelihood that two disputing parties will listen to reason decreases when anger is expressed during dispute resolution. Every workforce feels uneasy and is less likely to be productive when you always "crack" under stress. Consider the message sent to staff and whether doing so will produce positive and productive results before expressing a negative feeling.

2. Prepare yourself for events with high stress or tension

Preventing unpleasant circumstances or spending less time with people who trigger negative emotions are two of the most popular tips for avoiding bad emotions. For example, a leader may be unable to leave meetings or avoid workers and being forced to engage in or work with irritable people can worsen negative feelings.

A helpful piece of advice is to plan before doing something likely to draw criticism. Take several long breaths. Go into the scenario with an understanding of what you hope to do or achieve from it and be ready for any potential tension or disagreement. Accepting this ambiguity makes you more equipped to handle situations as they arise. You may be less inclined to react impulsively with rage or impatience when prepared for a possible confrontation.

3. Consider the implications

A brief negative outburst from you can have a long-lasting effect on the workforce. In times of change, employees look to you for leadership, and they can use any information from you—including your behavior—to make assumptions about your future. While expressing negative emotions may temporarily provide relief, employees look to you for guidance.

So you play a crucial role in establishing and preserving the organizational culture. When you express your rage or irritation, it can lead to a stressful work atmosphere where people are reluctant to share their thoughts out of fear of criticism. It can also foster intolerance and disrespect among coworkers. So consider yourself an example and recognize that employees will assess your words and actions.

WOMEN HELPING WOMEN

How to control and manage emotions while leading is a significant issue for women. But, unfortunately, we are condemned for expressing our feelings, even when we do so purposefully.

We occasionally feel that other powerful women don't support us personally or professionally. While we can't have all the answers to these challenges, I would like to share a few action steps that might be helpful.

Harnessing and Managing Your Emotions While Leading

Because of how we have decided to express our emotions in our professional careers as leaders and innovators—or, in some cases, how we have chosen not to express them—we have encountered judgment from men and women at various points in our careers.

But let's be honest—finding the right balance is something we all battle with daily. Our coworkers, friends, family, and even strangers often judge us. But it's crucial to recognize this judgment as it happens, use our feelings to our advantage, and control our weaknesses to move on more swiftly.

In essence, we've been taught that acting robotically and displaying little emotion will help us advance professionally and succeed faster. So, when we want to express true joy about something, we hold it in; we also control our disappointment or rage when a coworker doesn't deliver or meet a deadline and hide our tears by running to the restroom.

So what's the solution? One word—connection. The secret sauce I advise every woman to concentrate on when navigating the minefield of when and when not to express emotion in a professional situation is the cornerstone of all relationships. Maintaining a balance between being vulnerable and expressing emotion to others is a critical component of connection.

If you could build connections and feel proud of your accomplishments, you've succeeded and taken a step toward becoming a better leader. If you haven't, it is empowering to take a step back, reflect on the encounter, and acknowledge that it occurred before moving on. Do not linger or try to sustain a dead relationship. Instead, cut your losses swiftly and move on, whether in interpersonal interactions or tactical endeavors.

The relationships that value what you bring to the table as a strong leader should be nurtured and leveraged. I can attest that using a test-and-learn approach is incredibly awesome.

Pull Up a Seat at the Table for Another Woman

Honestly, there is no level playing field regarding how both men and women judge women. We are perceived differently and judged more stringently. Although more women are getting to the highest ranks in business and boardrooms, it is still fundamentally more challenging for women to ascend those ladders because it's still very much a man's world.

How, then, do you compete against all odds?

It's time for us to take action and focus on things we can do and behaviors we can alter since getting angry, annoyed, upset, or depressed isn't helpful.

Initially, you should gather allies rather than treat other women as rivals. Women have traditionally competed with one another; that's how we were socialized from the beginning of grade school. However, changing the game is the only practical way to alter the ratio.

Stop judging other women based on factors like being younger, prettier, more experienced, having a better job, or being more successful in their professional or private lives. Instead of competing with other women, we need to start supporting each other by creating networks, developing other women, and enlisting the assistance of benevolent males as allies. The goal is to assist other remarkable women in climbing the ladder rather than tossing the ladder aside after reaching the top position.

How We Can Help Each Other Rise

It's never enough to just understand or talk about a problem if we want to deal successfully with it. We have to break through the issues by attacking them with targeted actions. So let's examine even more detailed tactics we can use to help each other rise.

1. Take ownership of your emotions

It's ok to feel what you feel. All feelings are a part of what makes us human. So pay more attention to your feelings because they reflect how you are treated and your response to this treatment.

You need to own your emotions, even the negative ones we already discussed. That way, you can control your feelings and deal with any situation.

2. Help other women; let's feed each other

Men make friendly introductions to one another and engage people who may one day be able to assist them. They know by doing this, their networks or connections will grow and increase, potentially helping them in the future. On the other hand, women frequently approach situations from the opposite angle, delaying introductions out of concern that they could come across negatively. Or that they would lose their chances and places as a result.

166 | DAHLIA CALLUM

We need to act from a giving attitude of connectedness to prosper and build a solid basis for the future. We also need to establish a much broader network of powerful women so that there are other women in the room than ourselves.

3. Give other women the benefit of the doubt

As I explained earlier, the harshest criticisms often come from other women. Even other males have said this, so we know it's true. Naturally, you have no idea what is going on in another woman's life. For instance, she might have had a terrible event that she can't discuss. She might have been fighting the same institutionalized obstacles against women that we all do, but maybe more so due to her race, socioeconomic status, age, etc.

So why not judge other women less harshly than you would a man? Also, consider whether any judgments you pass on others are problems you avoid facing within yourself.

Finally, it would help if you publicly and genuinely celebrated one another's efforts and accomplishments. Don't be that woman who cheerleads women without actually helping them. Instead, honor others when deserved, and ensure you put your heart into it.

SUGGESTIONS FOR IMPROVEMENT

The other aspects of emotional intelligence (EQ) depend on self-awareness, which is the cornerstone of emotional intelligence. As a result, developing your EQ begins with self-awareness, the fundamental building block, and progresses from there. You can start to control these feelings and actions if you are conscious of your emotions and the resulting behaviors.

Now, there are barriers to self-awareness, and research has confirmed it. Being emotionally intelligent is impossible without clearly understanding your personality and motivations.

Ninety-five percent of participants in research by Tasha Eurich rated themselves high grades for self-awareness. However, the study indicated that using more empirical measures of self-awareness, only 10–15% of the cohorts were self-aware.

You'll agree there's a sizable discrepancy, implying that most of us aren't remarkably self-aware. Even worse, research suggests that managers and CEOs may possess the lowest levels of self-awareness overall. This is not in defiance of their authority but perhaps due to it.

In the Harvard Business Review, Eurich argued that people are more likely to be overconfident about how well they know themselves and their level of influence. After all, the people at the top of the chain receive less input.

When managers get feedback from staff, it's usually not as candid as it could be since subordinates are worried about suffering repercussions because managers are shielded from criticism, and their level of self-awareness declines.

Gaining self-awareness requires honest, helpful feedback. In addition, taking an emotional intelligence test can be a very efficient approach to learning more about your EQ traits and how you affect others.

But before we proceed to discuss the steps to improving your emotional intelligence, I'd like to share some of the signs of high and low EQ:

- **People with low EQ:** They often become overwhelmed by emotions, feel misunderstood, get upset quickly, and have problems being assertive.
- **People with high EQ:** They know the connections between their feelings and actions. They can persuade others to share the same goals while maintaining composure under pressure. They are also capable of handling challenging people with tact and diplomacy.

Three Steps to Improving Your Emotional Intelligence

Although many books have presented these concepts and cited the current research, the truth is that developing emotional intelligence is an ongoing process, and the journey differs from person to person. So I've outlined steps you may follow to improve and lead with emotional intelligence.

- **Recognize and name your emotions:** What feelings are you currently experiencing? Can you identify them? What feelings often surface in stressful situations? How would you prefer to react in these circumstances? Can you pause, think, and respond differently? An essential first step in EI is taking a moment to acknowledge your emotions and control your reactivity.
- **Ask for opinions:** Ask your boss, coworkers, friends, or family how they would grade your emotional intelligence to check your self-perception. Ask them, for instance, how you handle disagreement, how adaptable or empathic you are, or how you handle challenging situations. Even if it might not always be what you want to hear, it's usually what you need to hear.

- **Listen closely and withhold judgment:**
Strong, active listening abilities and an effort to
see the world from others' perspectives are the
first steps in the process. To foster a culture of
open communication and psychological safety
at work, pay close attention to what they have
to say and consider it. Recognize the other
person's emotions and express them back to
them. Listen to the beliefs and sentiments that
underlie the facts as you listen. Inform them
that you genuinely understand their emotions
and ideals by expressing your understanding of
those emotions.
- **Connect with employees personally:** You lead
with emotional intelligence when you show
that you care about your employees as people.
Also, your willingness to assist and
acknowledge their efforts will create room for
improvement. As a result, this gesture of
concern increases the trust between managers
and their staff.

As a performance metric, empathy has long been
considered a soft ability that is disregarded. But
according to my research, today's influential leaders are
more "person-focused" and friendly in the workplace,
which helps them get along with people from different

teams, departments, nations, cultures, and backgrounds.

- **Activate motivations:** Even if pay and benefits are significant, other factors also motivate and retain personnel. These advantages are a component of a more comprehensive motivational formula. Asking your staff and paying close attention to their answers is usually all it takes to figure out what drives them. Likewise, understanding your employees' motives will help you to improve retention, job satisfaction, and employee engagement.
- **Read literature:** According to studies, reading fiction with nuanced characters can increase empathy. It can assist in improving your social awareness to read stories from other people's viewpoints because it gives us a better understanding of their motives, ideas, and behaviors.

In the end, you would be surprised how you come off as approachable if you develop your EQ, as you will find yourself often smiling and radiating positive vibes. You will also leverage appropriate social skills based on your relationship with whomever you are around and know how to communicate clearly—verbally or nonverbally.

And before you know it, you will become a role model for those around you and inspire other ladies to think big. People are frequently motivated to act when they witness others who are similar to them doing so. Women are more willing to volunteer when they see other women in leadership positions because it makes it simpler for them to picture themselves in those positions.

7

BREAKING THE CYCLE OF GENDER BIAS AND DISCRIMINATION

"No country can ever truly flourish if it stifles the potential of its women and deprives itself of the contribution of half its citizens."

— MICHELLE OBAMA

Because many men and even some women hold prejudices against women leaders, women have difficulty obtaining high leadership positions. Too many people—both men and women—believe that women are passive, gentle, and sentimental and lack the masculine leadership qualities of being active, competitive, independent, and self-assured.

Unfortunately, these prejudices harm women's careers and encourage discrimination and gender bias in the workplace and business.

For instance, you could see a man and a woman from the same sales team work together to win the sale. But then, the company gives the man all the praise and even increases his pay later. In contrast, the woman's salary stays the same. And when she questions that, the usual excuse is something like: "Your numbers just weren't there." Then, she gets thrown aside when she further queries the reasons for not getting the credit for the sale like her male counterpart. Also, they tell her it's a team effort, and she should work on being a competitive and better team player.

Although the statistics on the extent of gender bias and discrimination against women may seem alarming, they may even be higher than we think. This concern was put to the test by two researchers from the psychology department at the University of Düsseldorf by combining two distinct questioning methods. One was the Direct Question (DQ) method, in which respondents answered questions with either "true" or "false" responses. The Crosswise Model (CWM) used an indirect questioning technique that randomly generated responses to ensure those survey responses could not be linked to specific respondents. There was a prediction that this feature would significantly reduce the need for respondents to modify their responses to fit social norms.

After conducting the poll, the researchers found that women were less prejudiced than men against women leaders. However, when given greater anonymity, more women than men were willing to declare their gender prejudice (using CWM). In conclusion, gender bias significantly impacts women more than men.

Unambiguous gender bias against women leaders is found in the research, with 28% of women and 45% of men expressing it when their identity is protected. This finding indicates that nearly one in two men and almost one in three women think men make better leaders.

The rise in bias, particularly among women, when asked indirectly about their bias as opposed to explicitly about it, suggests that prior surveys on gender bias using direct asking approaches underestimate the problem's severity and, consequently, the difficulty of eliminating it.

Despite the belief that most employees, supervisors, and senior leaders are objective, research suggests that gender bias and discrimination are particularly true of women in the workplace and business. You can also

176 | DAHLIA CALLUM

assume that measures like education campaigns and others to combat gender bias are successful when people just express what they think other people want them to say.

Therefore, the first step for women leaders to fight and reduce gender bias is to be aware of the impact of social desirability bias. And we must be more diligent and persistent in the battle against gender bias and discrimination, no matter what we hear. Fortunately, that's what this chapter covers; it reveals how you can fight against gender bias and discrimination in the workplace.

BARRIERS WOMEN FACE

According to a study by Susan Shortland of the International Journal of Human Resource Management, people who take on leadership positions frequently have prospects for career progression due to special stretch assignments. However, many top executives and managers don't consider women for an appointment due to cultural presumptions, organizational structures and procedures, and interactional patterns that unintentionally favor males and disadvantage women.

Despite being pervasive throughout organizations, it frequently goes unacknowledged and unnamed by both genders. It differs from overt and explicit gender bias because of its subtlety. For example, in the 1960s, a woman who became pregnant was usually fired; this type of gender bias was blatant and undisguised.

Today, unconscious and covert gender prejudice supports the patriarchal status quo by favoring men. It is an invisible bias that obstructs women's ascents to leadership and the development of their leader identities by prohibiting women from being seen as leaders and role models for other females.

Here are four instances of the various obstacles that women encounter:

- **Gendered work and career paths:** Male-predominant professions like computer engineering, architecture, and surgery are included in gendered career paths, and gendered work includes domestic and office duties. In my case, people weren't accustomed to seeing women work as salespeople in the automotive industry.
- **Double binds:** Women leaders often balance being perceived as either extremely feminine, which makes them appear friendly but less

competent, or overly masculine, which makes them appear competent but unpopular. However, women must be both competent and likable to succeed.

- **Women can't access specific networks and sponsors:** Compared to men, there are fewer sponsors or female supporters of women. Additionally, most women's networks differ from those of our male counterparts. Thankfully, we already covered how women can assist other women in business and the workplace in the previous chapter.

- **No role models for women:** Women have fewer chances to emulate people in senior positions who genuinely understand them. Men are overwhelmingly in high leadership roles across all sectors (private, public, and social). I dedicated the final chapter of this guide to this subject, as women need to start becoming role models for other women.

BREAKING THE CYCLE OF BIAS

In many businesses, discrimination against women still exists, whether intentional or not. It prevents women from rising to leadership positions, results in unequal compensation, reduces job possibilities, and occasionally leads to verbal abuse and harassment. We must first acknowledge that bias exists before trying to implement change. The following are several tactics for ending the cycle of gender bias in the workplace:

1. Bring the unconscious into awareness

Educating people about prejudiced behavior is a wise course of action. This usually entails learning to feel at ease during awkward conversations; taking improv classes and soliciting feedback from others are two strategies to practice. It might necessitate multiple discussions at times. Finding comfort in discomfort simply entails facing these difficulties head-on without letting them stop you.

Dealing with problems head-on also gives you power. Ask yourself, *"How do we all succeed?"* in direct response to the problem. How can we create an environment where people can flourish within the company? Since I feel this way, others will likely feel it as well, which is bad for everyone. So let's discuss it.

2. Manage how you are perceived by others and by yourself

To empower both yourself and others, you must use intentional techniques. For instance, if a younger female coworker accompanies you to an exclusively male event, you can place them in the middle seat at the conference table. If at all possible, give them a speaking role as well. That way, you will operate from a visual point of view and do your presentation without any pressure.

You should also know your strengths and weaknesses regarding what you can offer the company you work for. You must be the most excellent version of yourself, not someone else's idea of you, and be confident in your skill sets and what you bring to the table. Doing this is challenging, but it comes with knowing who you are, understanding your value, and having confidence.

3. Find allies, and be an ally

Everyone needs friends and mentors, but it's especially crucial for people aiming to succeed in fields with unwritten rules of success. Finding an ally can be beneficial in some circumstances, such as when male coworkers only converse with other males in meetings. For instance, whenever you are with a client who usually addresses only men, you can ask a subordinate male colleague to assist in rerouting inquiries to you in a meeting.

Finding methods to uplift others around us, bringing everyone into the conversation, and looking to your male mentors to offer the authority they almost exclusively possess due to their gender are all things we

THE BOSS CLUB | 181

should be doing. In addition, you will better cope with the larger context in the workplace by building connections.

Leaders who have attained success should spend time assisting those who came before them. Try to motivate, mentor, and give opportunities to younger female colleagues. Assign challenging projects to them and let them succeed and fail because you can also learn a lot from that. And these are all the main components of authentic leadership. Leaving behind even one of your less experienced employees could hurt your team's productivity. However, holding the door open will allow for collective progress.

Women experience various forms of racial and unconscious gender bias and discrimination. Unfortunately, these biases still affect women in the workplace, even though many businesses have demonstrated their commitment to resolving these problems by establishing family-friendly policies and fostering women's professional networks. Therefore, we must make an effort to fight against these biases to enable us to advance into leadership positions. Luckily, the rest of this chapter is devoted to solving these issues.

UNCONSCIOUS GENDER BIAS

Unintentional and involuntary mental associations based on gender derived from customs, expectations, norms, values, culture, and experience are called unconscious gender prejudice. On the other hand, decision-making is aided by automatic associations, which allow for a quick evaluation of a person's gender and gender stereotypes.

The International Labour Organization (ILO) Bureau questioned many businesses for Employers' Activities (ACT/EMP) to determine the biggest obstacles to women in leadership. According to the study, men's and women's societal roles were the second most frequently mentioned barrier. Additionally, respondents brought up the stereotype that management is a man's job. Finally, male-dominated corporate culture was the third most mentioned obstacle.

The respondents also mentioned negative gender stereotypes and ingrained bias against women in hiring and promotion. In general, discrimination and unintentional gender bias accounted for five of the obstacles to women in leadership.

For our study, here is an overview of how organization practices and other specific factors may hinder women's career advancement as unconscious bias:

1. Performance evaluation

Processes and programs adhering to stereotypically masculine standards always put women at a disadvantage and limit their chances.

Men's domestic responsibilities are also less demanding, facilitating their availability and geographic mobility. Therefore, this criterion penalizes women, especially working mothers, and has a pro-male, pro-childless bias.

2. Project assignments

Employees' visibility and ability to compete for promotion rise when they lead or participate in significant projects. There are two ways staff is assigned to projects. Senior executives or teams of employees are usually involved in assigning projects with high visibility, high implications, significant duties, and requiring highly particular skill sets or capabilities. Business unit managers or other designated workers frequently make selected assignments to lower-profile projects.

In either scenario, unconscious biases may impact the choice of who should be assigned to a project. These decisions may heavily rely on perceptions that emerge from stereotypical impressions rather than the employee's talents and worth if there isn't any experience or training to lessen the effects of gender discrimination among the staff.

3. Meritocracy

Performance is usually given top priority in organizations. However, the paradox of meritocracy is that employees who already have a lot of advantages may receive awards for excellent performance. And a performance evaluation based only on merit could exacerbate women's social or cultural disadvantages.

Additionally, managers could have false confidence in their ability to render fair judgments and may not know of the gender stereotypes they hold.

4. Leadership development programs

Even though participating in leadership development programs is essential for moving up the corporate hierarchy, men and women rarely have equal access to them. Senior leaders or people deemed to have high potential are these programs' primary target audiences. So these opportunities are only equally available to some employees.

Women had much fewer interactions with senior leaders than men. And as women advance in their careers, this discrepancy gets bigger. For example, only 51% of women in senior management, compared to 62% of males, said they engaged with a corporate leader at least once a week.

5. Norms

Workplace conventions may also hamper women's careers. For instance, the "think-manager-think-male" perspective is perpetuated when men only hold senior leadership positions, a common phenomenon.

Moreover, regulations like quotas may also (though not always) show that gender equality has advanced enough due to women's token presence, negating the necessity of continuing to strive to address the underlying problem of gender bias.

Assessing Unconscious Bias against Women at Work

The first step in overcoming the challenges mentioned in the previous section is to evaluate unconscious gender bias in an organization's operations and its effects on workers. You can employ several techniques, including perception surveys, linguistic analysis, analysis of gender differences in salary and career advancement, and even conducting tests.

Below is a description of each of these techniques:

1. Perception surveys

Collecting information on people's experiences is one of the most popular ways to evaluate unintentional gender bias at work. For instance, a perception study of Australian women working in science, technology, engineering, and mathematics revealed that 70% of participants agreed that unconscious bias had hampered their ability to advance in their careers and reduced their earnings by 60%.

Four hundred managers from various industries participated in an Ernst and Young perception survey, with 40% of the managers coming from India, Europe, the Middle East, and Africa, 30% from North America, and 30% from Asia and the Pacific. Men cited unconscious bias as the main obstacle to women's career advancement.

2. Language analysis

Nowadays, it is rare to find job descriptions that state the ideal candidate's preferred gender (though it still happens in some places). Even if a job description may not be overtly sexist, it still has the potential to reproduce and support gender stereotypes subtly. For instance, specific terms linked to prevalent gender stereotypes can indicate unintentional gender bias.

According to a study done in the U.S., males are associated with words like aggressive, domineering, achievement-oriented, self-confident, rational, and tough. In contrast, women are associated with words like emotional, mild, pleasant, sensitive, warm, and friendly.

Male applicants may benefit from an unconscious bias in their favor if leaders and job descriptions for leadership roles in an organization use any of these words frequently associated with the male gender. In contrast to women, men would be seen as having a natural aptitude for the position due to unconscious bias.

Beyond job postings, gender bias in language also affects other forms of communication. For example, Catalyst, a leading research and consultancy firm, examined data from 110 organizations spanning 19 different industries from their human resources systems (the research featured interviews, analyzing the documents of some participating companies, and an online survey). The analysis revealed that documents from human resources focusing on senior leadership roles were likelier to display stereotypically male characteristics than other human resources documents.

3. Analysis of gender gaps

Unconscious gender bias can affect how prospective employers evaluate parents applying for jobs. For example, an analysis of these discrepancies may reveal the effects of unconscious gender bias.

According to a study that compared equally qualified candidates, mothers were significantly less likely to be recommended for employment or, when they were, they were given starting salaries that were, on average, $11,000 less than those of candidates without a kid. Contrarily, fathers received significantly higher pay offers than childless men and were not penalized compared to them. This discrepancy raises the possibility that working mothers, in particular, are subject to prejudice.

In corporate positions that are requirements for leadership positions and executive management, such as line functions, a gender imbalance has been noted (positions with profit-and-loss responsibility or a focus on core operations). Fewer women continue on the route to the highest level of management due to the tendency of women to move from staff responsibilities (positions in human resources and public relations) to line duties at more senior levels.

4. Experiments

With the help of a specific scenario or data set, you want to ask respondents to express how they perceive gender.

The case study "Howard vs. Heidi" examined the trade-off between competence and likeability for female leaders. The study asked participants to assess a candidate's efficacy and competency, alternately presented as Howard or Heidi. Everything else stayed the same.

The subjects gave the candidate known only as "Howard," a venture capitalist, ex-entrepreneur, and skilled networker, a high rating for competence and effectiveness. Additionally, they liked him and were open to hiring or working with him. However, when given identical data for a candidate named "Heidi," the participants gave her a different rating. Although Heidi was competent and productive in their eyes, they didn't like or want to work with her.

It is acceptable to infer a gender bias that high-achieving women are less likable than high-achieving men, given that gender was the sole variable in the case study. While entrepreneurship, self-assurance, and vision are praised in men, they are seen as conceit and self-promotion in women. When women work in roles viewed as typically male, the trade-off between success and likeability becomes more pronounced.

Mitigating Unconscious Bias

Unconscious gender bias can exist in both individuals and organizations. So let's look at the steps leaders can take to prevent unconscious gender biases from influencing an individual's decisions.

1. Objective personnel decisions and talent management

Companies must ensure that hiring and promotion processes extend equal opportunities to men and women. The following describes measures that can help leaders in organizations reduce the impact of unconscious gender bias in critical workforce management processes:

- **Blind evaluation:** Hiding a job applicant's physical attributes can prevent implicit bias from influencing the selection process. It's an easy way to minimize bias, and fortunately, several online recruitment platforms have software to help companies see past physical attributes and improve the hiring and evaluation procedure.
- **Structured recruitment and performance evaluation:** A structured recruitment process is crucial to minimize the impact of unconscious gender bias in hiring decisions. Structured interviews, for instance, ensure all candidates are evaluated according to relevant and predetermined criteria related to work

performance. Comparative evaluations of the candidates' answers according to explicit standards can help to reduce gender bias and enable hiring authorities to choose the candidate with the best performance easily.

- **Transparency and accountability:** Your organization can adopt an utterly transparent career advancement process in which employees self-assess their progress and determine steps they should take to develop the skills and experience for promotion to the next level. You can implement this and other initiatives to ensure a broad pool of candidates is considered for promotion and evaluated objectively.

2. Using data

Unconscious bias can be revealed by analyzing data patterns and identifying gender gaps. Then, these gaps can be assessed as potential areas for intervention. However, stereotypes and prejudices can make it difficult to objectively determine and make inferences about the observed outcomes.

Large organizations with data analytics capabilities increasingly turn to data to identify gender inequalities and overcome these obstacles. For example, Google examined employee data and found that female employees quit the company at twice the average rate. Employee turnover is costly, so Google wanted to reduce the rate.

However, further data analysis revealed that it was, in fact, young mothers rather than female employees in general who were twice as likely to quit. This insight drove Google to introduce a new maternity and paternity leave plan. The plan has had a significant impact, as new mothers working at Google are now less likely to leave than the average employee. Google has since identified five indicators most predictive of turnover and has targeted its interventions accordingly.

3. Training employees

According to McKinsey and Company, almost all companies offer anti-harassment/discrimination training, but fewer offer employee training to eliminate bias in hiring (67%) and performance reviews (56%). Employees who don't understand how bias works are less likely to identify it themselves and make fair and accurate decisions. So they are less likely to push back on the bias when they experience it.

Even if training on unconscious gender bias is in place, it may not be executed appropriately. The insights of experts on this topic indicate that training aimed at promoting awareness of unconscious bias is generally insufficient to overcome it. The training must be complemented with capacity-building so that people can learn strategies to mitigate the impact of their unconscious biases. It must also offer support to those trying to tackle their unconscious biases.

Overcoming Gender Bias

In this section, we will explore the two methods for reducing the impact of unconscious gender bias in the workplace.

1. Analysis

It is no longer a debate that unconscious gender bias doesn't have a one-size-fits-all solution. Instead, effective interventions depend on the situation and difficulties the business faces. So you want to evaluate structural elements that socio-psychological research has identified as crucial to the emergence and upkeep of gender stereotypes. These include the following:

- **Industry and size of the organization:** Although an organization's size doesn't directly increase risk, it can affect how other risk factors interact and how well human resource management strategies work to achieve change.

- **Percentage of men and women in each division, across all organizational levels, and overall:** Stereotypic bias is likelier to occur where there is a gender imbalance in the workforce. Generalizations about gender's role in determining which persons may do particular jobs may come from gender stratification, where leadership positions are held by one gender and support positions by the other.

- **Practices in human resources:** Relevant aspects include implementing human resource programs to enhance recruiting and promotion processes and performance evaluation techniques in the current efforts to become more inclusive (for example, whether there are objective and unambiguous evaluation criteria). Personnel, committee gender composition, and training are further pertinent factors. The research will need access to the participating companies' performance management documents to analyze human resource practices accurately.

- **Organizational climate:** Mainly norms related to the "ideal worker" and a leadership ethos that fits the company's values.

Using evaluation tools, you can identify priorities and track qualitative and quantitative indicators to evaluate an organization's progress toward gender diversity goals. One of these tools is the Stereotypes Diagnostic Instrument, with which Catalyst helps its member companies assess their risk level and select intervention priorities.

2. Training

Your organizations can also offer specific training to businesses on unconscious biases based on gender or something else. The typical structure of training programs includes:

- Identifying implicit and structural biases in the organization
- Illustrating the impact of the bias
- Providing training participants with the knowledge and tools they need to identify and combat their own unconscious biases

Your organization can make the training available to employers free of charge and provide a complete set of tools and resources for a training workshop on unconscious gender bias.

Providing case studies can also help the training participants better understand and identify unconscious bias and adapt their workplace culture, processes, and practices to promote gender balance.

ADDRESSING RACIAL BIAS

Racial biases are biased beliefs that are both conscious and unconscious and have been formed through time based on stereotypes and frequently unfavorable opinions of one or more racial groups.

In addition to race, other intersecting identity markers such as gender, age, gender identity, appearance, perceived socioeconomic status, disability, nationality, ethnicity, and accent also impact these prejudices. However, race is the main element determining these prejudices.

Throughout my career, I have observed and overheard others discuss their encounters with racial bias and discrimination in the workplace. They consist of the following:

- Promotions and high-profile opportunities are not given to Black and colored personnel despite their comparable qualifications and, in some circumstances, greater experience than their White counterparts.

- Employees who are Black or racialized aren't invited to informal networking events.
- Employees who identify as Black or racialized may experience microaggressions, such as offensive jokes about race-based sex, being referred to as a "girl" or "boy," racial slurs, or mimicking accents or mannerisms in social situations at work or during team meetings.
- Black and racialized women often hear comments like "fix your hair," " tidy your hair to make it look more professional," "remove the dreadlocks," and other offensive remarks regarding how they look.
- When Black employees complain about unfair treatment at work, White coworkers and some racialized peers accuse them of "playing the race card."

Identifying Racial Biases in the Work Environments

Black and racialized employees suffer physical and mental health consequences due to racial bias and systemic racial discrimination in the workplace. Additionally, recognizing one's racial biases can be tricky and emotionally taxing.

It would be best if you urged the individuals you lead to participate in an introspection process. This process typically entails taking a close look at oneself, one's identity, values, and internalizations of other racial and ethnic groups outside and within one's social identity groups. Throughout my profession, I have had to integrate a process of introspection. And you can learn about your racial biases using online tools like the one developed by Project Implicit.

Employees are responsible for speaking out and reporting an incident if they observe racial prejudice at work. In practice, it is often tricky. When they have the opportunity, staff should speak up immediately, encourage the victim, and inquire about the next line of action.

You have more responsibilities if you are a manager or leader. It would help if you vigorously enforced anti-discrimination, anti-harassment, and workplace safety policies and self-reflect. You must comply with this legal and professional obligation.

What Can Companies or Organizations Do?

Let's say you own a business or company by creating multifaceted organizational responses to workplace racial prejudices, including effective workplace anti-racism and anti-oppression methods. In that case, you can eliminate racial discrimination, racism, and anti-Black racism and lessen racial bias.

Some of the successful strategies you can try include the following:

- Hiring a third-party consultant to help with the creation, development, implementation, and evaluation of workplace anti-racism and anti-oppression strategies which have lived experience and extensive practical knowledge in the areas of critical race, anti-Black racism, anti-racism, anti-discrimination, and organizational development.
- Auditing company policies and practices while watching out for discrimination and prejudice. Examining the hiring, retaining, promoting, job-evaluating, and firing processes is crucial.
- Creating comprehensive, well-funded programs for leadership and all employees' professional development.
- Giving young people and adults from underrepresented groups onsite and online internal possibilities.
- Discussing the company's efforts to combat anti-Black racism and racial discrimination during team meetings, annual general meetings, and other workplace gatherings.

Employers must also watch out for remarks and acts that, despite good intentions, undermine attempts to remove racial bias.

Below are some things you should avoid doing in the interim:

- Using a color-blind strategy (anti-racism tactics are undermined by claims that one "sees color").
- Denying racism's existence or pervasiveness or arguing that it should not be a discussion point.
- Asserting the idea that everyone should be treated equally is sufficient to end racism,
- Making the argument that whereas White personnel can be neutral and objective when talking about racism, racialized people cannot.

Suggestions for Improvement

Finally, let us look into more practical solutions you can use to fight racial bias and discrimination. These solutions are suggestions from different Black women on how to fight against racism and bring lasting change to our communities.

- **Support Black-owned businesses:** Do it for the culture! Supporting Black-owned women's businesses is becoming increasingly necessary.

Aside from healing systemic disparities, supporting Black-owned women's businesses will help keep money in the community, strengthen local economies, and close the economic wealth gap by increasing revenue and creating jobs. It will also provide examples of leadership for other women in current and future generations.

- **Educate and fill your shelves with these books:** Whether you are in management or involved in leading a particular department, you should not hesitate to educate yourself on systemic racism and gender inequality. The following is a list of must-read books I recommend:

  - *The Moment of Lift: How Empowering Women Changes the World*, by Melinda Gates
  - *Invisible Women: Exposing Data Bias in a World Designed for Men*, by Caroline Criado Perez
  - *Work Like a Woman: A Manifesto for Change*, by Mary Portas
  - *The Authority Gap: Why Women Are Still Taken Less Seriously than Men and What We Can Do about It*, by Mary Ann Sieghart
  - *Rebel Ideas: The Power of Diverse Thinking*, by Matthew Syed

Remember, educating your children about race is never too early or too late.

- **Interrupt your implicit bias:** Although bias is devilishly hard to eliminate, it is not as challenging to interrupt. The first step is recognizing how prejudice manifests in ordinary workplace interactions. Afterward, identify when and where these prejudices occur daily. Ignoring them is easy in the absence of an organizational command.
- **Spend more time listening without shutting down:** As discussed in Chapter 5, effective communication consists of two components: expressing yourself and listening to others. But, unfortunately, many leaders are less concerned with the second part. Indeed, many leaders are excellent communicators, but when it comes to considering the thoughts and feelings of others, they fall short. However, although listening can be pretty difficult, several people have the skill naturally. So it would be best if you were more deliberate in improving your listening abilities.
- **Redshift your thinking to facts, not assumptions:** When you assume gender bias doesn't exist in your organization, you do so without checking any evidence that it does.

Sadly, assumptions will only impede your ability to think creatively and solve the issue. Therefore, you must make a redshift from assuming to relying on facts. That way, you will discover perspectives that open rather than close possibilities for gender bias in your organization.

- **Create an activism plan:** Another tip for dealing with gender bias and discrimination is creating an effective activism plan. You can complete the plan yourself or have your colleagues complete it together.

- **Ensure your hiring practices are diverse:** A diverse workforce benefits everyone—and it's not just good for your business; it *is* good business. In fact, according to a study by McKinsey, companies with racially diverse teams tend to outperform others lacking in diversity—up to 35%. So it would be best to incorporate this practice too.

- **Expand your circle:** Whether you want to advance your career or meet new people to hang out with, you must learn—and perhaps master—the skill of making friends. Yes. You should learn to connect with new people and establish yourself as a value giver. But before spending more time meeting new people, do some preliminary planning. Determine the type of people you want to hang out with. Make a list of qualities, personality traits, or interests you admire, and don't be afraid to be a little more ambitious than usual.

Gender and racial bias are now more widely recognized as persistent issues in our society due to the tragedies and protests we have seen this year across the United States. As a result, we now have to decide if we will put in the effort required to alter ingrained attitudes, presumptions, policies, and practices.

Contrary to society, the workplace frequently necessitates interaction and collaboration amongst people from various genders and racial, ethnic, and cultural backgrounds. To break the gender bias and discrimination cycle, leaders should hold open and frank discussions about how their companies are doing so. It would help if you also used your influence to push for significant and ongoing improvement.

It might be challenging to "grin and bear it" while dealing with difficult people and battling against gender bias and discrimination. Yet, even when you are not with them, the memory of a particularly terrible person or interaction can linger in your mind. And this can hurt your mental health.

So what can you do to lessen such people's impact on you?

Fortunately, the next chapter provides insight into unpleasant people, how to identify them, and strategies for dealing with them both in business and the workplace. But before we dive into all that, what are some ways you can improve?

8

DEALING WITH DIFFICULT PEOPLE (WITHOUT HARMING YOUR MENTAL HEALTH)

"Always remember that you can explain things for people, but you can't comprehend for them."

— SHANNON L. ALDER

There will always be unpleasant or toxic coworkers. Developing the ability to deal with challenging coworkers, supervisors, customers, clients, and friends is essential. Indeed, dealing with complex situations at work is rewarding but challenging.

Working in toxic circumstances presents a double challenge for women leaders. They have to figure out how to deal with a hostile environment on one side. But on the other hand, they must maintain composure when managing their teams. Without realizing it, some women could exacerbate unfavorable workplace cultures.

You can significantly enhance your workplace and morale by developing your capacity to interact with coworkers. When you deal with the issues a tough coworker is causing the team; you also improve the working environment for all your employees.

You're not alone if you have a coworker who is toxic or proving difficult to deal with in the workplace. According to a study by leadership development consultancy Fierce Inc., four out of five employees either work with or have previously worked with a coworker who might be deemed toxic to the workplace. Too frequently, this behavior is accepted. Compared to the 88% of employees who would fire a toxic team member, only 40% of managers say they would.

This chapter discusses the steps that female leaders should take to identify and steer clear of toxic work situations while accepting personal accountability for their influence as leaders.

WOMEN LEADERS AND TOXIC WORKPLACES

When coworkers, managers, or the corporate culture creates a hostile work environment, it makes it difficult for people to work and advance in their careers.

The intricate web of the company's workgroup cultures, work processes, working environments, and social interactions is called the psychosocial work environment. Psychosocial safety also includes the absence of dangerous threats that could hurt one's mental and emotional health. Social relations in businesses include workplace bullying, sexual harassment, and other forms of emotional abuse.

Workplace Bullying's cofounder and director, Dr. Gary Namie, lists the following psychological risks that businesses should know:

- Hostile workgroup and organizational culture
- Overwhelming workload
- Violence, sexual harassment, and bullying at work
- Lack of rewards and recognition
- Lack of management or peer support on a social level
- Lack of control or excessive control over how work is performed

- Absence of involvement in decision-making
- Negative management and leadership
- Job instability

How Does Toxicity Impact Women?

Female leaders indeed confront many more obstacles at work than their male counterparts. When they consistently feel like they don't belong, many women lose faith in their ability to contribute. It is even more challenging for women of color. According to a McKinsey study, women of color continue to have worse work experiences than White women because they are more vulnerable to the adverse effects of discrimination and unconscious biases.

Most of the writing on female leadership focuses on changing women's behaviors. While this strategy enables women to take control of what is within their power, it only addresses one side of the problem. Women of color require an environment that promotes the inclusion of racial and gender identities and where everyone feels appreciated and celebrated to succeed in the workplace.

The Roles Women Play in Toxic Cultures

Women are present on both ends of the pendulum. Positively, women behave in ways that seem to fit preconceptions that place them in the category of having more socially acceptable traits than men, such as being likable, sensitive, and supportive of others.

For instance, according to the McKinsey survey, more women than men are taking the initiative to support their teams by acting more consistently to advance wellness. In addition, they offer assistance to team members in overcoming work-life conflicts and burnout.

DESI (Diversity Emerging Scholars Initiative) programs, such as supporting employee resource groups, planning events, and hiring from underrepresented candidate pools, are also being implemented in the workplace by more women.

Contrarily, there is a negative swing in the way some female leaders behave at work. According to the 2021 WBI U.S. Workplace Bullying Survey findings, women bully other women twice as often as males.

Additionally, female leaders with high perfectionism tendencies damage their colleagues by setting unattainable goals. Other female leaders are difficult to satisfy and are always unhappy with their team's performance.

All of this is to indicate that excessive proclivities can cause women leaders to stumble. They will remain unaware of how their actions and behaviors affect their team and continue to foster toxic work environments unless they become conscious of this impact.

WOMEN VS. WOMEN RIVALRY IN THE WORKPLACE

Women live under the scarcity principle because we have been positioned in society for hundreds (or even thousands!) of years: "there isn't enough for everyone; therefore, I must work extra hard to acquire mine."

Regarding career, female rivalry at work is fueled by competition for the few high-ranking positions women hold. For this reason, many women adopt the notion of "*if she succeeds, there's less chance I will also succeed.*" There aren't many successful women at the top, which shows why some women need to eliminate or undermine their "competitors." Simply put, they don't believe there is enough to go around.

Of course, women can be outstanding leaders and role models. But because we have yet to figure out how to get assistance from other women, that's one of the reasons there are so few women in these roles. Instead, we see one another as a threat.

It's Time to Break the Cycle of Female Rivalry

By first asking yourself the following questions, you can identify any hidden prejudices you may have:

- Do you hold other women accountable for decisions they individually wouldn't make?
- Do you punish women for minor offenses but pardon men for serious ones?
- Do you collaborate more with your male employees than you do with females?

It would help if you tried stopping the cycle of female rivalry if you answered *"yes"* to any of these questions. Here are the steps to follow:

- Support women by being a mentor or an advocate and creating opportunities. You can change how women interact at work by demonstrating there is space for many. For instance, don't judge a woman if you see her struggling. Instead, ask her how you can assist. Share information about your project accomplishments and the strategies you use for building successful relationships.
- Increase the chances of other women being heard in meetings by amplifying their ideas and proposals. Ask a woman to continue her

thought if she gets interrupted during a session. That way, she has the opportunity to speak, saving you from having to call anyone out.

- Give women credit for their innovations, achievements, and contributions. Recognize and applaud successful women in meetings, over email, and even in informal settings.

- Host a brown bag lunch, then invite other women to attend if you have highly sought-after skills or knowledge. Or start a book group for women to get to know one another and develop relationships if that seems too much work. Women benefit greatly from their casual relationships when returning to their formal workplaces.

- Join forces with other women to make your needs at work known. Working together has been shown to impact leaders and bring about change. Join the employee resource group (ERG) if only your organization has one. Discuss problems affecting women in your ERG and brainstorm ideas to present to your sponsor. If there isn't a forum for women at your firm, create one yourself.

- Do not disparage other women, spread rumors about them, or put them in the wrong. Instead, talk to them politely and frankly if you have any helpful criticism for another woman—not about them, but with them.

- Don't ignore an offensive joke or remark that you overhear. Even simple questions and responses like "What did you mean by that?" or "I didn't find that funny" can stop inappropriate behavior. You can do this more easily when the remark isn't made in your direction.

- Women's issues can be known in company suggestion boxes and leader Q&A sessions. Encourage others to follow your lead.

- Stop expecting more from female employees, colleagues, and direct reports than from male counterparts. Likewise, stop applying a double standard when criticizing women, including yourself. Instead, assume the best, and ask questions if something about their behavior puzzles you.

- You can always learn more from experienced people around you. Reach out to your female friends who have more life experience and discuss the challenges they have faced and overcome with them. They'll be grateful that you asked.

- Don't unintentionally haze other women by forcing them to go through the same struggles you did throughout your career if you've already "made it." Instead, reverse the elevator's descent.

- By enrolling in your company's mentoring program, you can offer to mentor the women around you. Create a program if your employer doesn't already have one or arrange casual lunch or coffee meetings with mentors. If you want to mentor several people, consider joining a mentoring circle.

- Post hours during which ladies can consult you for guidance. So many women merely require a confidante or sounding board. Make it a point to become familiar with the high-potential women in your immediate environment so that you can speak up for them regarding promotions and salary raises.

- Even though female rivalry is painful, it makes up a sizable portion of the professional connections with most women executives. In the end, recognizing unhealthy relationships is the key. You can still recognize the warning signs even if your circumstances are unchangeable. Also, look for strong, admiring ladies who want to be your mentors or sponsors. Find ladies who support you, don't see you as a threat, and want you to succeed. I promise you; such ladies exist.

HANDLING DIFFICULT COLLEAGUES

Most of us have encountered challenging employees or bosses at higher levels. Some of us may even have had others label us as problematic.

According to research, unfavorable stereotypes about women are prevalent concerning disputes at work. For example, in a 2013 study from the Sauder School of Business at the University of British Columbia, participants were asked to rate one of three work-place conflict scenarios. The only difference between the scenarios was the names of the people involved: Adam and Steven, Adam and Sarah, or Sarah and Anna.

Which one was viewed in the worst light? That's right —Sarah and Anna. Unfortunately, this perceived bias may impact how you act at work.

According to a meta-analysis of conflict styles, men lean more toward competition to resolve a challenging problem. In contrast, women lean more toward compromise. And when there is genuine cooperation, compromise is excellent.

Conflict avoidance is not a good thing. Avoiding arguments and keeping things silent leads to needless complexity and anxiety. Unfortunately, conflict avoidance is a problem for many women, even though it is not a uniquely female quality.

Therefore, you'll need to add to your arsenal of leadership talents if you work with challenging employees or bigger bosses. Fortunately, you can improve your ability to deal with problematic employees at the workplace. The tips below will help you deal with difficult people you'll encounter at work:

1. Negative coworker

Some coworkers spend all their time being negative. Both their employment and working for their company are unappealing to them. And they constantly work for lousy, jerkish bosses that mistreat them. Every workplace has some unpleasant coworkers; you know who the ones in your workplace are. Usually, avoiding these toxic coworkers at work is the best way to deal with them.

You can also maintain close contact with employees around the organization. Check for complaints, monitor employee intranet discussions, manage the appraisal and 360-degree feedback process, and teach people within the organization about proper staff treatment. This information helps you recognize the signs of negativity before its demoralizing effects harm your workplace. It will also help you prevent and reduce workplace hostility.

2. Get over your aversion to confrontations and conflict

Although confronting a coworker is never easy, it is often necessary if you want to defend your rights at work. Sometimes you need to confront a coworker, whether it's about giving each other credit for the job done, annoying or careless behaviors, willfully missing deadlines for client deliveries, or maintaining the progress of a project.

3. Develop effective work relationships

The relationships you form with your coworkers at work can harm your career and employment. If you can't get along with your coworkers, you will always have issues; it doesn't matter how much knowledge, experience, or authority you have. Therefore, establishing strong relationships at work to thrive in your profession is crucial.

4. Learn how to handle challenging conversations

Have any situations of dealing with challenging coworkers come up for you? It may be a coworker constantly bringing personal concerns to work or chewing gum loudly. Or an employee has poor personal hygiene or gives off an odor of liquor at work. These are only a few examples of behaviors that beg for thoughtful criticism from a coworker or employee.

You know the issue and productivity killer these personal and behavioral problems may be in your job. However, when you handle these sorts of challenging conversations correctly, it can result in beneficial outcomes.

5. Team building with coworkers

You want allies who have influence and will speak up for you before people the company views as their superstars. You can attain job security if your organization eventually sees you as a superstar.

Forming alliances is wise and valuable when you want to foster productive working relationships. These relationships are also essential for managing problematic or harmful workplace conduct among coworkers. They are also necessary if you want your ideas to be implemented.

6. Managing gossip

Most workplaces have a rife gossip culture. People usually act as though they have nothing better to do but engage in gossip. They talk behind one another's backs about their supervisors, coworkers, and the future of their business. They often exaggerate a truth that is only partially accurate compared to its significance or intended meaning. Dealing with challenging rumors is both necessary and possible. So endeavor to eliminate harmful rumors and gossip from your workplace.

DISCIPLINING VS. FIRING AN EMPLOYEE

Being let go shouldn't ever come as a surprise. You should never fire any employee unexpectedly unless your company has been the target of a hostile takeover fit for a pirate or a 60-minute exposé that brings the villagers with torches and pitchforks. Every terminated employee should be aware of their likelihood of getting fired and be prepared to accept responsibility when it occurs. There shouldn't be any surprises.

But when is it appropriate for you to fire a worker, and when should you look for ways to help them get better? Of course, when firing an employee is necessary, you must handle it properly, respectfully, and with dignity. But often, when considering firing someone, you might pass up a chance to change the problematic behavior and keep a good employee on the team.

Josh Bersin of Bersin by Deloitte claims it takes a new worker one to two years to restore their previous productivity level, and training can cost up to 20% of their annual compensation. So finding the right balance between the work required to address issues with the benefit of regaining a valuable employee and the benefit of avoiding the need to invest time, effort, and money in replacing them is the secret.

Below is the first factor to consider while deciding whether to fire someone:

You employed that person because you believed they had potential. Unless they grossly exaggerated their abilities and knowledge, they were probably once a valuable team member. So would it be worthwhile if you could solve the issue and return them there?

Managers complain about having to discipline staff. *Why do I bother the staff about issues when they are adults who know what is expected of them?* It's unpleasant!

However, staff employees see a lack of correction as tacit consent. The stunning outcome is frequently the unanticipated "you're fired" down the road. Instead of saving that employee with a few easy steps of accountability and correction, you start the employee turnover cycle (and costs) all over again.

Let's look at a few scenarios of problem employees and examine whether they should be saved or sacked.

Unpunctual Joe

Joe usually arrives late for work. He does an excellent job but needs to be punctual. He's highly competent at his job, but you get annoyed when he routinely arrives late to the daily staff meeting, and you have to give him separate updates. Is it worth trying to retain this employee?

Every time you see him slipping in late, you give him the stink eye and leave notes on his desk telling him to "make an effort to arrive to work on time," but because it makes you uneasy, you avoid sitting down and having an honest chat with him. Then, he commits to improving, which he keeps for a few days before reverting to his old habits. So what do you do?

Progressive discipline might be effective for Joe. Remind him that the rules still apply to him just like they do to everyone else, regardless of how excellent his work is. If he doesn't accept responsibility for his faults and make it right, he will be dismissed—yes, fired! Use your progressive discipline policy and adhere to the first, second, third, and termination phases.

The challenging part now is that you must adhere to it. Joe must be fired if he can't arrive on time. Any employee unable to uphold the terms of employment should be subject to the same policy. They must assume accountability for their errors and responsibility for their future career. If they are unable to, then the outcome is their fault. That's it!

Of course, firing him without trying to improve his unpunctuality would be unwise. However, if you've told him about the issue, given him multiple warnings, and he still arrives late, be ready to take the awkward action of terminating him. The morale and output of your team may depend on it.

Hushed Jenny

Jenny suffers from severe public speaking anxiety. She is brilliant and has many creative ideas, but sharing them with anyone, even a small group, makes her nervous. She stumbles and becomes disoriented in the background noise when she is asked to talk. The group believes they are carrying her, and that Jenny isn't helping.

You feel you might have to sacrifice her for the greater good since resentment causes strife on the team.

Can you insist that Jenny overcome her public speaking apprehension immediately and subsequently? That might be a tall effort, given that speech anxiety affects 75% of Americans. However, Jenny can be introduced to group talks with some work. You already know what the team will debate, so meet with Jenny in advance and take down her suggestions. Offer your opinions throughout the discussion, mentioning that you contributed the ideas during a different meeting. If the team has any questions, try to respond to them yourself or, if she can, defer to her. She might feel more at ease and be more able to participate as her ideas catch on and become accepted.

Then, privately follow up with Jenny. Congratulate her on her successful ideas or discuss the ones that failed. Give her a place to speak freely and leverage each opportunity to bolster her self-esteem. The goal is to increase her comfort level and get her on board with the group. Spending the time and effort necessary to keep a talented employee is beneficial.

It is possible to change the habits of many competent workers, though it can be costly and taxing for HR and other related departments. The same goes for getting new employees. That's why most organizations treasure proficient employees who understand the corporate culture and don't necessarily require training. However, you are responsible for recognizing and correcting any bad habits an employee may have that are hurting the team as a whole.

Tell-Tale Signs an Employee Should Be Fired

Joe and Jenny are two workers who can be saved, but others may not be worth the effort. So when is it appropriate to fire a worker? Here are several warning signals that a worker has to go:

- **Adverse actions are not corrected:** Rules are not advice. If employees have had enough time to address issues but still need to, they should look into other career options.
- **They impact the mood:** Although the office bully may have a client list as long as his ego, their negative personality traits affect everyone interacting with them. Even though you might feel like you can't let them go, think about how morale improves while they are on vacation. Wouldn't it be lovely if life were like that every day? Bid your farewell!
- **Their actions reduce productivity:** Can't accomplish anything because "someone" hasn't finished their portion of the project once more? If repeated reprimands and increasing repercussions have failed, it's time to hire a professional.
- **They lack motivation:** Why do you care about them if they don't care about the job, the client, the business, or coworkers? If you can't

change their attitude, it's time to turn them over.

- **They love conflict because it makes for good theater:** They take advantage of any chance to criticize the organization, thrive on office turmoil, and feed off bruised feelings. They initiate fights and then watch them unfold. If you ever wanted to bother, you're not qualified to handle these personality problems. Remove the tumor they've developed into, then allow recovery to start.

- **They commit serious offenses:** Some corporate policies call for an immediate and final reprimand in the form of termination. There are no progressive disciplinary measures for theft, no "three strikes and you're out" for bringing a weapon to work, and no escalating repercussions for using drugs while at work. Such transgressions call for immediate dismissal. Remember that this doesn't go against the principle that no employee should ever be shocked by their termination. They should know the weapon/theft/high policy and the consequences for breaking it and be ready to accept the punishment they have earned.

- **They are that person:** One more type of employee you should fire as quickly as possible is the person who first comes to mind as deserving of termination. If you've given this person countless chances and given it a lot of thought as to how, why, and when you should let them go, the chances are that the moment has come.

You may argue that everything is excellent, but firing people is awful. However, it can be beneficial, quick, and easy if done correctly. It should take at most ten minutes to fire someone. Yes, you heard correctly: an average separation should take no longer than ten minutes.

SUGGESTIONS FOR IMPROVEMENT

Nobody intentionally creates a toxic corporate culture, and often there isn't a quick fix that you can use to correct one. When top leaders fail to enforce compliance for offenders or when there aren't any policies to guide behavioral standards, women may lack the social capital or influence necessary to change the culture in toxic workplaces. However, they can still take action to solve their predicament and choose how to better represent their interests and those of the teams they manage.

If some of this information strikes a chord with you, various helpful strategies for navigating challenging workplace cultures exist. Consider your team, the organizational context, and the environment for the best approach and action plan.

Outside Your Team

- Keep an eye out for the characteristics of social interactions at work. Recognize the prevalent, undesirable behaviors. Then, be honest by outlining them and acknowledging how they affect you.
- Analyze your level of safety at work.
- Reframe how the negativity around you affects you. Having a leadership coach by your side helps keep you grounded. In addition, you can learn how to develop your resilience with the aid of a coach.
- Never lose your voice, no matter how hard this is. Be prepared to speak out.
- Connect with your needs and ideals but recognize your limitations. Set limits and use the word "no" as required.
- When someone pushes your boundaries, think about documenting the improper behavior and be prepared to report it.

- Find supporters from the highest levels of management who will stand by you and support you.
- Know when enough is enough. Sometimes, the only way to handle intolerable situations is to leave.

Learn through reading and education. Knowing more will keep you in control and enable you to continue acting as a change agent for the better. Here are some resources to help you learn more about this subject:

Inside Your Team

- Describe the kind of leader you wish to be in your vision. Think about your advantages.
- Choose one or two behaviors you wish to work on and commit to doing so daily. Small, steady steps can take you far. To assist you in your efforts, think about working with a coach.
- Recognize and accept responsibility for any ways you may be fostering a toxic culture. For instance, if you are a perfectionist leader, learn to delegate more and minimize the number of revisions.
- Try to create a supportive environment for your staff. What I suggest are the following:

1. Make errors and poor decisions acceptable.
2. Acknowledge reasonable efforts and express individual gratitude.
3. Set an example of good habits.
4. Be open and honest.

Knowing your values, strengths, and areas for improvement will help you stand tall even when confronted with a toxic atmosphere as a female leader. Even if there may be many reasons for becoming a victim, it will benefit you to use your inner resources and take action from a position of empowerment.

Women leaders also have the power to gradually change hostile work settings into ones that value dignity, respect, and inclusivity. And for this reason, it can seem natural to use women leaders as role models for younger women to emulate.

Cognitive psychologist and organizational development expert Laree Kiely has this to say: "At the root of almost all conflict is who gets to tell who what to do." First, you need to identify a point of agreement for both parties to avoid such an issue. After that, you can address the problem by framing it as a concern rather than a difference of opinion. The final phase is to increase your influence so that the other person views you as an example and is inspired to seek your counsel.

It is conceivable that seeing women in leadership roles can aid in combating toxic workplace environments, dispelling harmful preconceptions, and promoting greater gender equality. Being a role model is the seventh of the successful leadership approaches, so I've decided to focus on it in this book's next chapter.

9

BECOMING A ROLE MODEL AND INFLUENCING OTHER WOMEN

"A role model should be like the light at the end of a tunnel, guiding you when you are lost."

— CRISTINA IMRE

M oses, Alexander the Great, Marcus Aurelius, George Washington, Abraham Lincoln, Winston Churchill, Mahatma Gandhi, Martin Luther King Jr., and Ronald Reagan: We have forty centuries of history conditioning us to think of men when discussing role models.

For most people, women included, the word *leader* or *role model* carries masculine connotations. But that is changing. Just look at Indra Nooyi, Theresa May, Hillary Clinton, Oprah Winfrey, and the likes. Indeed, this trend is so lovely to see.

Now, don't get me wrong. I'm not the type to talk down to men. But I am only contending that we need women to rise and take places of leadership alongside men.

We need to focus on the powerful and effective style of leadership centered very much on openness, trust, teamwork, relationships, and empathy—attributes that are core strengths for many women. Most organizations and businesses will significantly benefit from such leadership. And frankly, I believe the challenges we face as a culture demand it.

Therefore, we women need more role models. The lack of female role models is one main reason women do not have the confidence or just try to avoid certain management positions and leadership roles in business and the workplace. Our focus in this chapter is on what being a role model involves and how you can become one to help you inspire others and influence productivity at work.

FUTURE OF WORK

Female business executives are shaping the future of work today. Indeed, everything is changing, from how teams work to how managers keep staff members motivated and satisfied. Companies are also changing their perspectives on work-life balance, gender diversity in the workplace, and how to develop the next generation of leaders effectively.

These shifts present an enormous opportunity for enhancing how we all work, and women in business are seizing these opportunities. Three significant ways that female leaders are transforming the workplace are outlined below:

1. Female business leaders raise the bar for employee treatment

When employees transition from the physical office to remote work in today's world of remote work, they develop new needs. Employees who work remotely need the same management and support as those who work onsite.

Thankfully, female managers are stepping up to provide their workers with the encouragement they need to succeed during the transition. As you already know, women tend to be more empathic, which helps them understand their staff members even when they are not physically with them. As a result, women in management roles are changing how managers encourage employee engagement and productivity.

2. Female business leaders redefine work-life balance

Female executives must rethink how they interact with their staff and make time for self-care. Women who thrive in the remote work era must reevaluate their expectations for work-life balance.

We put a lot of pressure on ourselves to excel as parents and leaders at work. We experience all the feelings and worries our loved ones, coworkers, and colleagues experience. And it's incredibly overwhelming to feel that weight and strain all the time.

However, female leaders avoid burnout by focusing more intently on their needs. It's okay and recommended to take breaks from work. Indeed, we must spare time for ourselves to maintain our energy. Women who manage simultaneous caregiving responsibilities renegotiate expectations at work and home.

3. Companies must empower the next generation of women

Even though I've made it to the top, there is still a sizable gender gap in senior leadership positions throughout the corporate sector. So today's female executives and their organizations must take a proactive stance to increase the number of women in the C-suite.

This discrepancy will continue if it's not actively addressed. And that's because businesses that employ fewer women have fewer possibilities to foster the advancement of the subsequent generation of female executives.

The next generation of female leaders must come from a pipeline of early- to mid-career women. So, yes, women must receive early career help.

Younger women in the workforce benefit significantly from the mentoring of current female CEOs. However, organizations also need to set up processes to promote female talent. But, unfortunately, this shift cannot occur naturally for another ten years. So a clear and focused plan must come from the leadership.

Companies that employ female-specific training programs assist women in developing early career skills and confidence, positioning them to assume leadership roles later. Also, these businesses are putting themselves in a better position to enhance gender representation throughout their whole organization and the business sector by increasing the number of women in leadership positions.

GROWING YOUR INFLUENCE

Even while the inherent barriers women must over-come to pursue leadership positions are increasingly dissolving—albeit too slowly—many still find the journey extremely difficult. However, women may find supporters, develop ideas, and acquire respect from coworkers, bosses, and peers in the sector using their influence. Generally, influence opens up opportunities for participation, expertise delivery, and recognition while paving the way for leadership.

So anyone who wishes to market their ideas and objectives to others must understand leadership. In the end, people use influence, which is the ability to affect agendas and outcomes and win over others to accomplish their goals. We all know influencers because we regularly and closely observe them in action. Moreover, those who are genuinely influential among us exhibit exceptional skills that support and maintain their success.

However, in a male-dominated company, women can struggle to use their power. But you can still surmount these challenges despite this.

Below are a few tips for increasing your power at work:

Be Known for Reliability

Authority is demonstrated through words and deeds. You demonstrate dependability by excellently and creatively completing tasks on schedule, which increases your authority. Generally, your dedication reflects well on you and has just as much sway as your views. So others may rely on you for advice and to deliver in a pinch if you are known for your unshakable dependability.

Nevertheless, being dependable does not require you to accept some tasks. Saying "no," although it may seem paradoxical, enables you to address your tasks with care and give them the attention they require. Women in the workforce often believe increasing their work-load or providing assistance whenever needed will increase their influence and establish them as capable handlers of enormous responsibility.

However, refraining from overcommitting yourself and establishing your credibility requires you to say "no" when you know you can't do something and do it well. It is simply unreliable to produce subpar or delayed work due to being overworked. So be picky about the tasks you accept, and don't hesitate to decline other offers. It will be challenging to exert authority if you constantly commit to every task, never present new or improved perspectives, or never differentiate yourself from the crowd.

Be Confident as an Introvert

Did you know that quiet leaders can have just as much impact as loud ones? Well, now you do. Another quality that might be a strength for leaders is the capacity for stillness. Many individuals find silence uncomfortable and want to fill it with impulsive remarks, whereas the comments an introvert offers can be considered more. And being considerate can undoubtedly lead to influence.

The key is being at ease with your communication and leadership styles, regardless of whether you are outgoing or introverted. There may be circumstances where you need to be open, vulnerable, reticent, direct, or display other attributes that can all be incorporated into your leadership style. Being quiet doesn't change the game but understanding when to open up and foster confidence and trust does.

Be Assertive

Teams are practical organizational tools, but they can also be their worst enemies, which is why it's so crucial for women in leadership to be proactive and increase their impact. You should promote your ideas and forge consensus within teams to establish your authority and get outcomes that boost your influence.

Influence, however, goes beyond just you; even when working with or as a team, listening to others and bridging gaps in views may increase your leadership. Employees and coworkers who know they can approach you do so with confidence in your ability to impact them, and you ultimately gain from their mutually beneficial support.

Without a doubt, women leaders and those aspiring for administrative or executive positions face many difficulties. However, increasing your influence is a strategy to overcome such obstacles and be prepared to face future ones that will inevitably appear. Ultimately, a clear long-term win-win situation is one in which increasing influence advances your career.

WOMEN LEADERS INFLUENCE PRODUCTIVITY

Women are often attributed to having superior soft skills and higher emotional intelligence (already discussed in Chapter 6). Giving women in businesses and organizations more opportunities to hold leadership positions may boost productivity and improve financial results.

Women are likelier to notice when a coworker has personal problems limiting their productivity; for instance, they are more inclined to initiate a conversation to find a solution. They also provide a remarkable ability to "read the room" and detect the energy in a social or professional setting. Women are likelier to address a problem or settle things amicably before getting to business.

A lack of gender diversity can have the same adverse effects on a workplace environment as a lack of cultural diversity. Successful businesses know different perspectives, ideas, and insights can combine to enhance creativity and improve problem-solving. Men and women each bring unique skills to the workplace. And these advancements have a direct impact on productivity, which then results in higher profitability.

Therefore, you should not feel less competent than your male counterparts because women have a distinct advantage in building relationships, motivating, encouraging, and mentoring others. And with such a great advantage, women leaders can increase productivity and earnings.

Now, let's discuss ways you can improve your team's productivity and efficiency as a woman boss.

1. Give your team members ownership

The most effective corporate executives know the importance of ownership. However, giving team members ownership only entails empowering them to take charge of their actions and holding them responsible for the results of those actions.

A team member held accountable for their job develops a sense of ownership. As a result, they approach their work differently so that their choices can improve the team's overall effectiveness.

Giving ownership can take many other forms, such as taking charge of a project or task. When you give team members ownership, you show confidence in your team members' competence to handle a particular task. And as a result, you realize that no strategy improves productivity better than boosting someone's self-esteem.

2. Ensure proper communication

Another critical element that significantly boosts team efficiency is communication. Businesses fail without efficient communication, as I discussed in Chapter 4. And since miscommunication results from a lack of communication, this usually leads to failures across a business's arms.

Communication is crucial for team members to understand their work responsibilities. So any communication problems can cause misunderstandings, affecting the team's productivity. Thus, consider developing programs or courses to keep everyone in line, whether you need to onboard new staff, provide employee training, or have a place to save crucial information.

3. Identify your team's strengths and weaknesses

A manager or team leader is responsible for identifying their team member's abilities and skills and considering them when assigning duties. Indeed, knowing each team member's skill set is essential to creating an effective team.

For instance, you could force a team member who enjoys coming up with original ideas to present them to a client. Team members look forward to contributing to the workplace because they are confident they use their skills, knowledge, and abilities to the fullest extent possible. Using their talents will help improve and increase your workplace's productivity.

4. Team building exercises

The level of camaraderie among team members significantly impacts the team's productivity. So the office atmosphere will improve if the team members get along and know each other's talents and flaws. When team members are content inside, productivity and efficiency inevitably increase.

There is a chance that not everyone in a team will get along. However, you can use team building exercises to reduce conflict among the team members. That way, resentment and misunderstandings among team members will be cleared up fast and easily.

5. Use a project management tool

Today, no one can dispute online project management software's contribution to increasing collaboration and output. The appropriate project management tool can facilitate efficient time management and improved teamwork. Several online project management tools are available, so feel free to check and pick the right one.

6. Create a wholesome work environment

Infrastructure and work conditions are key factors in increasing team productivity and efficiency. According to a recent study, the workplace's physical environment largely affects how employees feel, think, and perform.

As a result, many businesses take extra care when designing their offices' interiors. They usually incorporate natural elements like plants and flowers, bright lighting, and cozy furniture arrangements. And like physical surroundings, the office environment also affects team productivity. An authoritative leader, condescending workers, and office politics can hurt an organization's total production and efficiency.

7. Reward your employees

Employees perform at their best when given a motive to work, most likely a financial motive. They desire to receive more from their superiors than just a pat on the back because they want their efforts recognized and rewarded. To maintain employee motivation, a lot of employers implement incentive programs.

A recent study found that offering an incentive made 85% of the workers feel more motivated to work hard. These rewards include cash, gift cards, extra time off, lunch outings, etc. So I hope you're taking note, leaders.

8. Give employees room to work

When given the freedom to complete tasks their way, every employee or team member performs at their best. Unfortunately, most employees lose interest when their supervisors or employers micromanage them.

Making an awesome team is one of the many strategies to help you overcome this. First, give team members a detailed explanation of their duties and your expectations. Then, get out of their way so they can work independently. Also, be personable so your team members won't hesitate to ask questions when confused. Finally, always have complete faith in your staff. This further increases their self-confidence, which boosts their performance.

9. Praise a job well done

While you may need to combine various strategies to increase some employees' productivity, for others, the ideal strategy is as simple as giving them credit for their work. Nothing can increase productivity if employees feel their contribution isn't valued enough. So praising their efforts, especially in front of the entire team, can be very effective.

This outward display of gratitude encourages individuals to perform to their highest potential better than merely offering simple congrats. It also promotes a positive workplace culture, which will help to increase team productivity.

10. Give constructive feedback

If employees don't know they're inefficient, they can't hope to improve. So giving constructive criticism is vital to improving team productivity. In addition, learning about the areas of opportunity will inspire team members to modify their working methods.

Ask your team members what you can do to help them improve after giving them feedback. They may prefer more direction on some tasks or a little more room for creativity. This promotes an atmosphere of open communication that will make future partnerships simpler and more fulfilling.

SELF-ADVOCACY AND RESILIENCE

You require more than just technical expertise to succeed in business. To be a successful leader, you must combine knowledge with skills. Self-advocacy and resilience are two of the most critical leadership traits and are vital for women who want to manage and lead.

Self-Advocacy and Its Importance at Work

Self-advocacy is the capacity to speak up for yourself in the broadest sense. It's the capacity to recognize your needs, express them adequately, and explain how others may support you.

Self-advocacy is advantageous in all aspects of life. However, it's crucial in the corporate sector, where many tend to go with the flow to avoid upsetting people. Your professional life may suffer if you can't speak up for yourself. For instance, you can experience extreme stress, anxiety, burnout, and dissatisfaction with your employment. And unfortunately, these problems could prevent you from receiving a promotion or other opportunities and affect your work performance.

Self-advocacy increases understanding; it also alerts people to your problems. There's a strong probability your peers won't be aware of your challenges if you never speak out. However, speaking up for yourself and expressing your needs enables your team to start addressing gaps, issues, and roadblocks earlier. This is an essential component of success.

Developing your self-advocacy skills is critical to maximizing your career potential. It's one of the things that can determine whether you spend years in the same job or advance to management or another leadership position after a few years. Being a strong self-advocate enables you to express your desire for development and career advancement. Additionally, you can ask for what you require to reach your objectives.

Resilience and Its Importance at Work

Self-advocacy alone won't get you far in your career or help you succeed at work; you must also possess resilience. Resilience is the ability to recover from difficulties, setbacks, or other unanticipated situations that could otherwise result in issues. Essentially, it's the capacity to manage your problems and succeed despite them.

Fortunately, just like self-advocacy, you can learn how to be resilient. If you don't recover well right away, there are things you may do to improve your capacity to handle stress and prosper under pressure. Success will come as a result of doing this.

Resilience in the workplace involves more than just overcoming obstacles. Resilient people typically cope with stress better. As a result, they often have greater self-esteem and job happiness. Also, they are more invested in fostering productive working relationships and more engaged in doing so. Additionally, they can typically take criticism better and resolve problems more swiftly.

The benefits of building resilience extend beyond just you personally. For instance, being resilient allows you to help your coworkers more effectively, which can benefit your team and organization and increase your overall output.

Resilience can also improve your mental health and well-being at work. Absenteeism, presenteeism, and burnout are all associated with poorer mental health. With resilience, you learn to be more adaptable. That way, you can quickly adjust to changes in the workplace while still producing work of a high standard. Being resilient and leading by example can help you succeed as a leader.

In the concluding section of this chapter, I will share tips on how to build your self-advocacy and resilience skills to advance your career.

Empowering Mimicry

Several ethical and practical arguments favor increasing the ratio of capable, accomplished women in leadership roles. These ladies can positively influence women's conduct and aspirations for leadership by acting as strong role models.

Women imitate successful female role models' strong (open) body postures. This results in more empowered behavior and better performance on challenging leadership tasks, according to research that studied the behavioral process through which visible female role models empower women in leadership tasks.

Women need to see visible female leaders as role models because they can imitate their nonverbal cues, such as their commanding body postures. The process known as "empowering mimicry" occurs when women take on these assertive postures for themselves, furthering the empowering impacts on their performance.

Therefore, increasing the visibility of female leaders may be advantageous for women doing demanding leadership jobs. In addition, these female leaders can serve as role models for women by demonstrating how to act in difficult circumstances, thereby empowering women.

ROLE MODELS ARE KEY IN GENDER DIVERSITY

According to studies, encouraging women to make new decisions through role models is very beneficial. Their impact is founded on the idea that "seeing is believing," which is interesting because it operates on several levels.

Parents and peers see various options: others frequently sway women from choosing a particular path. At gatherings, demoralizing comments like "Gosh, an engineer? That's unusual" are often made to female engineers.

However, these comments are unhelpful. But these stories alter as others see more women thriving in such areas. For example, the same study discovered that parents were more inclined to urge their daughters to continue their education after witnessing at least two female chefs.

Women usually draw inspiration from others who act like them. When they see other women in leadership roles, it makes it easier for them to imagine themselves in such situations; thus, women are more willing to speak up and put themselves forward.

Therefore, working specifically on promoting role models is crucial. One way to do this is by promoting gender balance in the photos organizations share on their websites, social media, and business magazines. But it's also important to go past that.

Verify that the speakers, presenters, trainers, and forum participants are a diverse group of women and men. Likewise, verify the gender balance in the allotted speaking time as well. Then, consider ways to challenge gender stereotypes as you work to increase visibility purposefully.

SUGGESTIONS FOR IMPROVEMENT

It can be hard or uncomfortable to stand up for yourself, especially at first. Likewise, making your demands known could come off as complaining about your obligations or, even worse, showing that you cannot handle them. You might feel that keeping quiet is preferable but doing so can mean passing up opportunities. Ultimately, your career may benefit you if you speak up and feel confident.

Directing your professional development and accomplishing your goals requires actively advocating for your needs. So let's go over what you can do to improve your ability to speak out for yourself.

1. Recognize your worth

Self-advocacy involves more than just knowing and expressing your needs. It's equally important to recognize and express your value. You must be able to back up your request for a promotion or even a few extra duties by offering evidence of your suitability for the position. Write down the values you contribute to the company when you are ready.

2. Recognize your weaknesses

Consider yourself from your supervisor's perspective. Think about the reasons they might reject your application for a promotion or other leadership position. Consider what you can do to address those worries, then do it.

3. Improve your confidence

Others will only be confident in their talents if you are. You must have confidence in your ability to succeed if you want to speak up for yourself. Although you don't have to have the highest level of self-assurance in the room, increasing your self-assurance is essential to developing your self-advocacy skills. That could entail changing your inner dialogue, repeating mantras, or maintaining a list of your skills close at hand.

4. Look closely at your objectives

Taking on a leadership role impacts both you and your organization. You may demonstrate that giving you the position helps everyone by coordinating your goals with your organization.

5. Establish a good reputation

Your actions speak for you more than any words you could ever say. So you can showcase your skills and prove you are a team player by building strong working relationships with your coworkers. In other words, you can develop a reputation for being dependable, accountable, and diligent. And you won't need much effort to self-advocate because your actions will speak for themselves.

6. Declare your accomplishments (but do so carefully)

You risk never being seen if you wait for people to notice your successes. It's okay to inform your superiors or bosses about your dedication to your work. But there's a thin line between boasting and promoting your accomplishments. Praise your achievements, but tread carefully.

Similar to self-advocacy, only some are naturally resilient. However, it is a skill you may pick up and develop with time.

7. Develop grit

Expert on the topic, Angela Duckworth, defines grit as being passionately enthusiastic and driven to accomplish a certain objective. Someone with grit is so committed to achieving their goal that they won't give up in the face of difficulties or disappointments. Almost everything they do has a purpose concerning their goal.

There will be challenges on your way to achieving a difficult goal. But you can build the resilience you need to overcome those challenges by persevering in hardship.

8. Develop strong relationships

Resilience depends heavily on supportive relationships inside and outside the workplace. They act as a social support system. In trying or stressful circumstances, a network of dependable friends and coworkers can provide support.

9. Practice mindfulness

Being mindful is learning to be in the present; when you're mindful, you're conscious of your surroundings, actions, and emotions. Additionally, you aren't allowing stress to control you. Instead, practicing mindfulness enables you to monitor your thoughts and spot patterns that might impede your progress.

You can pause and objectively assess the situation to devise solutions by engaging in mindfulness practices. You shift from reacting to a stressor or challenge to responding to it when you exhibit mental agility. Take a moment to label your thoughts and emotions to activate critical thinking rather than emotional decisions.

10. Improve your balance

It can feel nearly impossible to strike a healthy work-life balance in a world where technology keeps you connected to your job twenty-four hours a day. However, taking advantage of that downtime to decompress and recover—or bounce back—is essential for building resilience. In addition, it provides you with the vigor you need to handle challenging work scenarios.

11. Keep your positivism

Optimists anticipate success despite challenging or demanding circumstances. Even amid uncertainty, keeping a positive outlook can inspire you and the people around you to take action and meet the problem head-on. It results in increased resilience, which raises optimism.

12. Be in charge of your emotions

You must be able to manage your emotions if you want to be resilient. To achieve this, you must become conscious of your sentiments and how you respond to them, both negatively and positively. You can better manage stressful circumstances by becoming more aware of your emotional state and better preparing for them.

Finally, I want to implore you to act as the mentor you wish you had when you started. Say "yes" if someone asks you to be their mentor. Say "yes" if you are invited to an interview. Say "yes" when asked to join a panel and ask another female to do the same.

Celebrate female leaders in your life and the news and be open about your leadership experiences. A young lady who reads or hears your story might be inspired to have more faith in herself than she otherwise would. She could recognize her potential and a route forward for a different future.

And if you hear a girl being referred to as "bossy" or "aggressive" or being blamed for asserting herself, step in and explain that she should be praised for her leadership qualities, not chastised. Make sure ladies understand the advantages of leadership, such as having a voice and influencing others!

HELP OTHER WOMEN TO FLY WITH YOU!

Now that you're a fully-fledged member of the Boss Club, you're well-equipped to help other women spread their wings and soar high alongside you.

Simply by leaving your honest opinion of this book on Amazon, you'll show new readers where they can find the guidance they're looking for.

MAKE A LASTING IMPRESSION!

Thank you so much for your support. Women are powerful... But we're even more powerful when we work together.

Scan the QR code below to leave a quick review!

CONCLUSION

"You gain strength, courage and confidence by every experience in which you really stop to look fear in the face. You must do the thing you think you cannot do."

— ELEANOR ROOSEVELT

First, let me congratulate you for finishing this book and taking the decisive step to learn how to become a more effective leader.

Like the air we breathe, there are some things we take for granted as long as they are present but greatly miss when we lose them. Leadership can be like the air— invisible but vital for business. And when it's not present, the organization begins to die. And that is why I tell aspiring women leaders the presence of leadership is not always known, but the absence of leadership is always felt.

When it comes to leadership, it all starts with determining your preferred style, and this depends on your personality and how you intend to manage your team or employees. Afterward, you must learn to use your secret weapon, your confidence. You will lay a perfect foundation for becoming a successful leader by finding it and building off of that. But it is worth noting that attaining confidence is half the battle; keeping it and living with confidence is the other half.

You should work on your decision-making skills. Do you know which principles matter to you the most? Examine your "code of ethics" for a while. If you know what matters most, making the right decision when faced with a moral or ethical option is likely to come naturally to you.

How well do you communicate and manage your emotions when dealing with your employees? As a leader, your communication skills should also be above par. You should understand and manage your own emotions and recognize and influence your employee's emotions.

Also, do not let gender bias thrive in your workplace. Bias and discrimination hamper the development of women's leadership identities. It accomplishes this by prohibiting women leaders from being regarded as leaders and role models for other women.

In addition, you must learn to deal with difficult colleagues and resolve conflicts between your employees, team members, customers, or vendors. Also, knowing when it is the right time to discipline or fire an employee is vital if you want to succeed as an executive leader.

Indeed, leadership can be invisible, just as leaders always fly under the radar. Leadership rarely involves standing up on a chair with a megaphone or running out ahead of the parade, waving one's arms like a majorette. And much of the most effective leadership has to do with the techniques we have covered in this book. Leadership is not as it appears but as it performs.

In other words, it doesn't matter which of these seven winning leadership techniques you adopt or whether it conforms to everyone's preconception about what leadership looks like. What matters is the outcome. Did your team accomplish its goals? Did you win in the end?

There is a growing appreciation for this truth, which is good news for women. It means we don't have to explain or prove that it's possible to lead without going overboard to meet a list of unfair expectations. We're entering an era in which the ability to deliver results trumps everything else.

One thing is sure, though: no matter the chosen leadership technique, women who lead successfully do so because they embrace leadership as a lifestyle. And you must do the same. You must also work hard to become a successful leader such that other women around you see you as a role model. Fortunately, by taking your time to read through this comprehensive guide, you have a head start!

Leadership is second nature to women because we are made for greatness. Don't let others tell you otherwise! You're a badass boss capable of doing anything within her grasp because you are a strong woman. So permit me to officially welcome you to the Boss Club!

It would mean a great deal to me if you could take some of your time to leave a review on Amazon with your feedback on the book, and if you liked it, then do tell your friends and colleagues about it.

I wish you all the best on your leadership journey.

Cheers.

Just For You!

Free Gift To Our Readers

Learn the 5 mistakes made by CEOS of the world's top companies and how to avoid them. Visit:
www.dahliacallum.com

REFERENCES

Adrian, H. & Jochen, M. (2019, January). *Gender bias against women leaders is higher than we think.* https://ideasforleaders.com/Ideas/gender-bias-against-women-leaders-is-higher-than-we-think

Andrews, S. (2022). *Gender barriers and solutions to leadership.* https://trainingindustry.com/magazine/issue/gender-barriers-and-solutions-to-leadership/

Ariel Blog. (2022). *Women and leadership: negotiating with the inner critic.* https://www.arielgroup.com/women-and-leadership-negotiating-with-the-inner-critic

Audrea, F. (2019, July 17). *The art of persuasion: every woman needs this skill.* https://www.thinktankofthree.com/2019/07/the-art-of-persuasion

BalanceGirl. (2022). *Why female rivalry in the workplace exists.* https://thewomenscode.com/female-rivalry-in-the-workplace

Banerjee-McFarland, S. (2018, September 12). *Women in leadership: growing your influence at work.* https://ideas.bkconnection.com/women-in-leadership-growing-your-influence-at-work

CCL Blog. (2022). *15 tips for effective communication in leadership.* https://www.ccl.org/articles/leading-effectively-articles/communication-1-idea-3-f

CCL Blog. (2022). *Emotional intelligence and leadership effectiveness: bringing out the best.* https://www.ccl.org/articles/leading-effectively-articles/emotional-intelligence-and-leadership-effectiveness

Carol, G. K. (2021, March 3). *Body language for women who lead.* https://www.koganpage.com/article/body-language-for-women-who-lead

Catherine. C. (2022). *Ten ways to boost your confidence as a woman leader.* https://thinkingchoices.com/ten-ways-boost-confidence-woman-leader

Colin, B. (2022, June 20). *Master active listening with these 11 techniques.* https://leaders.com/articles/leadership/active-listening

Crystal, R. (2021, April 16). *You're not a fraud. Here's how to recognize and overcome imposter syndrome.* https://www.healthline.com/health/mental-health/imposter-syndrome#takeaway

DeFrank-Cole, L. & Tan, S. J. (2022, March 1). *An invisible bias with real implications for women leaders.* https://blogs.lse.ac.uk/businessreview/2022/03/01/an-invisible-bias-with-real-implications-for-women-leaders

Donnell, R. O. (2022). *When (and how) to fire an employee: 7 signs it's time to terminate.* https://hire.trakstar.com/blog/when-and-how-to-fire-an-employee

Ellevate Network. (2019, December 23). *Secrets to confidence for every woman leader.* https://www.forbes.com/sites/ellevate/2019/12/23/secrets-to-confidence-for-every-woman-leader/?sh=66c6c5036fde

Forbes Coaches Council. (2020, May 28). *Top business and career coaches from forbes coaches council offer firsthand insights on leadership.* https://www.forbes.com/sites/forbescoachescouncil/2020/05/28/16-essential-strategies-to-improve-your-decision-making-skills/?sh=6de8895b6532

Harvard Blog. (2019, August 26). *How to improve your emotional intelligence.* https://professional.dce.harvard.edu/blog/how-to-improve-your-emotional-intelligence

Heathfield, S. M. (2021, February 2). *10 tips for dealing with difficult people at work.* https://www.liveabout.com/dealing-with-difficult-people-at-work-191790

IMD Blog. (2022). *The 5 most common leadership styles & how to find yours.* https://www.imd.org/reflections/leadership-styles

Indeed Editorial Team. (2021, April 26). *Why is decision-making an important leadership skill?* https://www.indeed.com/career-advice/career-development/why-is-decision-making-an-important-leadership-skill

Inge Woudstra, (2022, APRIL 11). *Role models are key in gender diversity – especially in tech & engineering.* https://www.shecancode.io/blog/role-models-are-key-in-gender-diversity-especially-in-tech-engineering

Jeff, T. (2022, February 3). *Communication skills for women leaders.* https://speechimprovement.com/communication-skills-for-women-leaders

Kara. (2017, July 13). *Powerful, confident body language for women.* https://www.executive-impressions.com/blog/powerful-body-language-for-confident-elegant-women

Kashyap, V. (2022). *10 ways to empower your teams to be more productive.* https://www.proofhub.com/articles/how-to-improve-team-productivity

Katie, S. (2022, October 4). *Great women leaders negotiate.* https://www.pon.harvard.edu/daily/leadership-skills-daily/great-women-leaders-negotiate/

Kevin, K. (2021, September 30). *Your team is judging you on these six emotions (and women are judged differently.* https://www.forbes.com/sites/kevinkruse/2021/09/30/your-team-is-judging-you-on-these-six-emotions-and-women-are-judged-differently

Kiner, M. (2020, April 14). *It's time to break the cycle of female rivalry.* https://hbr.org/2020/04/its-time-to-break-the-cycle-of-female-rivalry

Knight, R. (2019, January 28). *How to decide whether to fire someone.* https://hbr.org/2019/01/how-to-decide-whether-to-fire-someone

Kouchaki, M., OC, B., & Netchaeva, E. (2021, March 31). *Breaking the cycle of bias that works against women leaders.* https://sloanreview.mit.edu/article/breaking-the-cycle-of-bias-that-works-against-women-leaders

Larina, K. (2010). *Great leaders are great decision-makers.* https://gbr.pepperdine.edu/2010/10/great-leaders-are-great-decision-makers

Lauren. B (March 2, 2022). *Perfectionism: our dirty little secret.* https://wearegirlsclub.com/women-and-perfectionism

Lauren, L. (2019, April 3). *Why emotional intelligence is important in leadership.* https://online.hbs.edu/blog/post/emotional-intelligence-in-leadership

Leadership Articles.(2020, September 25). *5 ways to improve your leadership communication skills.* https://crestcom.com/blog/2020/09/25/improve-communication-skills

Little, N. (2013, October 17). *How to ... handle a difficult colleague.* https://www.theguardian.com/women-in-leadership/2013/oct/17/how-to-deal-with-difficult-colleague

Mind Tools Content Team. (2022). *Emotional intelligence in leadership.* https://www.mindtools.com/pages/article/newLDR_45.htm

Mind Tools Content Team. (2022). *Managing your emotions at work.* https://www.mindtools.com/pages/article/newCDV_41.htm

Mocafi Blog. (2022). Helping women bridge the gap: why you should support black-owned women businesses. https://mocafi.com/2022/03/08/helping-women-bridge-the-gap-why-you-should-support-black-owned-women-businesses

Morgan, B. (2021, March 7). 15 *of the world's most inspiring female leaders.* https://www.forbes.com/sites/blakemorgan/2021/03/07/15-of-the-worlds-most-inspiring-female-leaders/?sh=60162d2e3e6e

Paskin, B. (2022, March 24). 5 books to help you fight gender inequality. https://www.ourwhiskyfoundation.org/the-cut/5-books-to-help-you-fight-gender-inequality

Perez, M. J. (2022, July 24). *How women leaders navigate toxic workplaces.* https://www.linkedin.com/pulse/how-women-leaders-navigate-toxic-workplaces-mari-j-perez-pcc/?trk=pulse-article_more-articles_related-content-card

Pratch. L. (2011, November 28). *Why women leaders need self-confidence.* https://hbr.org/2011/11/women-leaders-need-self-confidence?registration=success

Press Room, (2018, November 10). *Business woman media: letting go of perfectionism to increase your effectiveness.* https://www.aboutmybrain.com/blog/business-woman-media-letting-go-of-perfectionism-to-increase-your-effectiveness

Prince, S., Layton, D. & Hunt, D. V. (2022). Why diversity matters. https://www.mckinsey.com/capabilities/people-and-organizational-performance/our-insights/why-diversity-matters

Rachita, S.(2022). *7 secrets for female leaders to boost self-confidence.* https://thriveglobal.com/stories/7-secrets-for-female-leaders-to-boost-self-confidence/

Relax Blog. (2022). *7 techniques for effective leadership negotiation process.* https://relax.ph/blog/leadership-negotiation/

Replicon. (2022, May 11). *17 reasons women make great leaders.* https://www.replicon.com/blog/17-reasons-women-make-great-leaders/

Sandberg, S. (2015). *Lean in: Women, work, and the will to lead.* Random House

Sanders, P. (2022). 6 tips for expanding your social circles. https://www.lifehack.org/articles/communication/6-tips-for-expanding-your-social-circles.html

Shana, L. (2021, December 2). *Women leaders: can we talk about feelings?* https://www.linkedin.com/pulse/women-leaders-can-we-talk-feelings-shana-lawlor

SIGMA Blog. (2022). *Great leaders have emotional control.* https://www.sigmaassessmentsystems.com/emotional-control

Signature Consultant Blog. (2022). *Women in it leadership: how to master your* Inner Critic. https://www.sigconsult.com/blog/2021/09/women-in-it-leadership-how-to-master-your-inner-critic?source=google.com

Sojourner-Campbell, T. (2020, June 11). *Addressing racial bias and discrimination in the workplace.* https://lifespeak.com/blog/addressing-racial-bias-and-discrimination-in-the-workplace

Soken-Huberty, E. (2021, March 26). 10 reasons why listening is important. https://theimportantsite.com/10-reasons-why-listening-is-important.

Tallon, M. (2020, February 4). *What is self-confidence and why is it important for women in leadership – part i.* https://moniquetallon.com/what-is-self-confidence-and-why-is-it-important-for-women-in-leadership/

Ndanu, E. (2022a, June 2). *Quotes on Effective Communication from Women - AWIT.* AWIT - African Women in Tech. https://www.africanwomenintech.com/quotes-on-effective-communication-from-women/

Thompson, A. (2021, June 16). *Future of work: how female leaders are transforming the workplace.* https://www.hrdconnect.com/2021/06/16/future-of-work-how-female-leaders-are-transforming-the-workplace

UAGC Blog. (2022, June 17). *4 leadership styles in business: leadership style quiz.* https://www.uagc.edu/blog/4-leadership-styles-in-business

Weingus, L. (2022, December 5). *20 habits of successful women.* https://www.silkandsonder.com/blogs/news/18-habits-of-successful-women

WomensMedia. (2016, November 2). *Using emotional intelligence is a woman leader's secret weapon.* https://www.forbes.com/sites/womensmedia/2016/11/02/using-emotional-intelligence-is-a-woman-leaders-secret-weapon/?sh=3f8ea95419f7

WorldofWanderlust Blog. (2022). *17 habits of highly successful women.* https://worldofwanderlust.com/17-habits-of-highly-successful-women/

Young Entrepreneur Council. (2017, October 3). *Eight traits every powerful female leader possesses.* https://www.forbes.com/sites/yec/2017/10/03/eight-traits-every-powerful-female-leader-possesses/?sh=335dc665608f

Made in the USA
Middletown, DE
25 August 2023